NORTH AMERICAN STEAM
A PHOTOGRAPHIC HISTORY

NORTH AMERICAN STEAM
A PHOTOGRAPHIC HISTORY

Marie Cahill & Tom Debolski

Introduction by Bill Yenne

BISON GROUP

First published in 1991 by
Bison Books Ltd.
Kimbolton House
117 A Fulham Rd.
London SW3 6RL

ISBN 0 86124 848 1

Printed in Hong Kong

*Page 1: A line-up of Pennsylvania Railroad
K4 Pacific 4-6-2s. The K4 was the Pennsy
passenger hauler in the last days of steam.*

*Pages 2-3: Southern Pacific No 4449 in
Daylight livery belches out a full head of
steam as it rounds a bend in the Siskiyous.
SP donated No 4449 to the city of Portland,
Oregon in 1958.*

*Below: No 5000, with a 4-10-2 wheel con-
figuration, was typical of the locomotives in
service throughout Southern Pacific's vast
network during the 1930s.*

Designed by Tom Debolski
Captioned by Marie Cahill

CONTENTS

INTRODUCTION
by Bill Yenne

Both rail transportation and photography were born in that innovative epoch in the early nineteenth century which saw the dawn of what has come to be known as the Industrial Revolution, that point which historians now refer to as the beginning of modern times. In a very real sense these two inventions formed the cornerstone for the two parallel technologies—mechanized transportation and optical imaging—that would define 'progress' over the ensuing two centuries.

Both rail transportation and photography were derived from experiments that dated from the dawn of the nineteenth century. The first successful steam railway locomotive was built by Richard Trevithick in Wales in 1804, while the camera lucida designed by William Hyde Wollaston in England in 1807 was the nearest ancestor to the 'camera photographica.' The camera lucida, unlike the camera obscura that dated back nearly half a millennium, was a convenient easy-base apparatus that was carried everywhere by fashionable ladies and gentlemen to record images of themselves and their travels, much as snapshot cameras are used today. The camera lucida had a glass prism suspended at eye level by a brass rod. Looking through a small hole at the edge of the prism, the user saw the subject and an image on drawing paper simultaneously.

Meanwhile, Thomas Wedgewood, of the famous English family of potters, had been experimenting with paper sensitized with silver nitrate since before 1802. He noticed that the nitrate-impregnated paper would turn dark when exposed to light, and that objects placed on it would render white silhouettes. Wedgewood never went further with his experiments but Joseph Nicephore Niepce and Claude Niepce, working in France between 1815 and 1827, combined Wedgewood's technique with a lens, the result being negative images which they called 'heliographs.'

Modern photography was born in 1829 when the Niepce brothers formed a printer shop with the theatrical painter Louis Jacques Mande Daguerre, although they did not perfect a practical technique for making photographs until 1837, and it was not until January 1839 that it was officially announced that 'M Daguerre has found the way to fix the images which paint themselves within a camera obscura, so that these images are no longer transient reflections of objects, but fixed and everlasting impress which, like a painting or engraving, can be taken away from the presence of the objects.'

Meanwhile, several steam-powered rail locomotives were built in England in the first two decades of the nineteenth century, including George Stephenson's locomotives built for the Hetton Colliery in England in 1822. Stephenson and his son Robert established a locomotive works at Newcastle in 1825 and went on to produce *The Rocket*, remembered as the first truly successful commercial locomotive, in 1829. *The Rocket* garnered the Stephensons a host of orders for new equipment from a growing Liverpool & Manchester Railway and the age of mechanized transportation had begun.

The pioneer American railroad built for general public use was the Baltimore & Ohio, chartered in 1827. Construction was begun in 1828, but apparently not on a large scale because only 13 miles were open for traffic in 1830. Five years later the length of the road was 135 miles. The first rail of this historic road was laid on 4 July 1828 by Charles Carroll, the only living signer of the Declaration of Independence. As Professor Hadley commented in 1855: 'One man's life formed the connecting link between the political revolution of the last century and the industrial revolution of the present.'

In May 1829 a new locomotive, purchased from George Stephenson at the Rainhill Trials, arrived in New York. As was the custom, the engine was cheerfully colored, including a bright red lion's head on the front of the boiler, to go with its name, the *Stourbridge Lion*. Shipping it west to central Pennsylvania, Horatio Allen, America's first engineer, proceeded to demonstrate its marvels. To the consternation of would-be passengers, the wooden tracks upon which the train was to travel ran across a 100-foot-high hemlock trestle bridge spanning Lackawaxen Creek. The seven-ton engine appeared far too heavy for the wooden span, which was considered safe for no more than three tons. Allen fired up the boiler, pulled the throttle-valve and headed off alone at 10 miles an hour. The bridge held, so he ran on happily for several miles, demonstrating to ecstatic farmers and townspeople alike the modern miracle of steam locomotion. Although the bridge had not collapsed, unfortunately the wooden rails had been somewhat chewed up.

Soon the wooden rails were retrofitted with metal bands. The Railway Age had come to America.

The history of North America's railroads is, to a certain extent, the history of North America's people and their desire to bind their continent with bands of steel

Facing page: A Union Pacific steam locomotive charges across the plains—like the buffaloes that populated the Great Plains before the arrival of the Iron Horse.

for the purpose of advancing their civilization and their standard of living. Historian Oscar Skelton compared the building of North America's rail network to the building of Europe's great cathedrals half a millennium before. In both cases it is hard to imagine the energy of the people who undertook such tasks with the limited technology available to them. In both cases it took the energy and commitment of thousands of people over many years to complete these monumental tasks, and it took the exceptional vision of a few to conceive and organize these projects. In the case of the great cathedrals, the names of the visionaries are lost, but in the case of the railroads the names of the empire builders are an indelible part of North America's history.

The construction of numerous other roads was begun shortly after work commenced on the Baltimore & Ohio. The South Carolina Canal & Railroad Company was chartered in 1828, and in 1834 it had 136 miles in operation. For a short time it was the longest line in the world under one management. The parent company of the New York Central system, the Mohawk & Hudson, was chartered as early as 1826, and began construction in 1830. The 17-mile line from Albany to Schenectady was opened in 1831, and five years later Albany and Utica had been connected by rail. In 1842 Buffalo was reached, and by that time lines had been built from New York and Boston to Albany, so that the east and west of that period had been joined.

Between 1830 and 1835 railroad building was pushed more rapidly in Pennsylvania than in any other state, and 200 miles were opened. The first division of the great Pennsylvania Railroad system was the Columbia Railroad, by which Philadelphia was connected with Columbia, on the Susquehanna River, in 1834. The road was built by the state after its construction was authorized in 1828. This railroad was a link in the through route consisting of canals and railroads that connected Philadelphia with the Ohio River at Pittsburgh in 1834. The line to connect Philadelphia with New York, the Camden & Amboy, was chartered in 1830 and completed in 1837. The road from Philadelphia to Baltimore, the Philadelphia, Wilmington & Baltimore, was chartered in 1831 and finished in 1837. The Reading Railroad, built mainly for the transportation of coal, was chartered in 1883 and opened for traffic five years later.

Americans began to build locomotives in 1830 at about the same time that they became involved in railroad building. The English locomotives were expensive, could not be secured promptly and when obtained were not well adapted to the light rails, steep grades and sharp curves of the American tracks. The traffic conditions caused the engines and cars to be built according to designs different from those followed in Great Britain, and the differences in equipment set the tone for the development of American rail cars for the next century and bequeathed to the nation a rail network that made such a vast contribution to North American civilization and economic growth.

At the same time, photography in general and the photographic documentation of railroads specifically, evolved at a rapid rate after Daguerreotype photography gave way to the much less fragile and more versatile calotype photography in the 1860s. To portrait and still life photography was added the art of location photography. Suddenly, exotic distant vistas were brought into everyone's drawing room. After the Civil War—which had been so vividly photographed by Matthew Brady—the great westward expansion of the United States brought with it the expansion of the national railroad network and this was duly documented by photographers. Alexander Gardner followed the construction of the Union Pacific as it progressed west from the Missouri River, and Captain Andrew Joseph Russell was present to capture the most historic photo of American railroad history (see pages 116-117) on 10 May 1869.

During the decade of the 1860s, the mileage of the railroads in the United States increased from 30,635 to 52,914. The rate of growth was slow except during the last two years of the period. From 1868 to the Panic of 1873–74 was a period of intense speculation and of very rapid railroad construction. Indeed, the severe business crisis of 1873 was largely the result of building railways too rapidly and of overcapitalizing those lines. During those five years following 1873 only 11,500 miles were built.

In 1880, there were 93,296 miles of railroad in the United States. This marvelous achievement was unparalleled in the economic history of any other country of the world. Within 10 years the people of the United States built as many miles of railroad as the people of the three leading countries of Europe had constructed in 50 years. The building operations were carried on in all sections of the country, but the largest increases were made in the central and western states, where settlers were rapidly taking possession of the unoccupied agricultural and grazing sections of the vast public domain, and where vast mineral wealth was causing cities and states to be established on the great Rocky Mountain plateau. Capitalists, confident of the growth of the county, and assisted by generous aid from the United States and from local governments and individuals of the sections to be served, constructed railroads to create the traffic upon which the earnings of the roads must depend. In many cases the railroads built during the 20 years following the Civil War were pioneers entering unsettled regions beyond the Mississippi and Missouri rivers and opening the highways by which immigration was able rapidly to occupy the prairies and mountain valleys of the West.

In 1906 there were 222,000 miles in the United States, nearly 40 percent of the railway mileage of the world. The mileage in the United States exceeded that in all Europe by more than 15 percent. By 1929 the total mileage had increased to only 229,530. By 1939 it had decreased to 220,915 and by 1980 to just 164,822. Thus, the turn of the century truly marked the point at which America's railroads turned from expansion to management of existing lines.

In 1844 Ross Winans of Baltimore constructed a locomotive with eight connected wheels. Four years later he brought out the first 'camel' type of engine, so named because the engine-drivers's cab was placed above the middle part of the boiler. The construction of mogul and consolidation locomotives became common after 1870.

During the last half of the nineteenth century a great many important improvements were made in locomotives. Among the most valuable innovations was the introduction of compound locomotives, by which steam, in passing from the boiler to the exhaust, was used in two cylinders in succession. By that means a greater amount of power is derived from a given quantity of fuel.

The steam locomotives in use in the early twentieth century weighed as much as 25 of the engines used at the beginning of railroading. A locomotive weighing 200,000 pounds was not considered notably heavy, and some with their tender weighed 500,000 pounds. In 1850 a locomotive weighing more than 50,000 pounds was considered large, and a train load of 200 tons would have been a heavy one to handle. Fifty years later, 2500 to 3000 tons were hauled over long distances by the largest of freight engines. The achievements in increased speed of locomotives were less pronounced, but the schedule speed of 60 to 65 miles an hour for passenger trains, regularly maintained on many American roads in 1900, was double the rate possible in 1865, and the discomforts and risks were less.

All this while, the locomotives were being documented by the manufacturers in photographs made with huge cameras producing 8-X-10-inch glass negatives. These side-view photographs, known as 'roster shots' were stunningly sharp and revealed the locomotives in minute detail. The huge Baldwin Locomotive Works in Philadelphia produced literally hundreds of thousands of locomotives and each one was methodically photographed. During Baldwin's halcyon days in the early twentieth century, Baldwin photographer Fred Haines personally documented over 25,000 locomotives.

In the 1940s steam locomotives began to be replaced by diesel locomotives. In 1948 as the greatest era in American railroad history passed into posterity, the Smithsonian Institution in Washington was given what is perhaps the largest collection of railroad photography in America, outside that of the Baldwin Locomotive Works. This collection was the result of the life's work of a man named CB Chaney.

Born in Baltimore, Maryland in 1875, Chaney was fascinated by railroads at an early age and although he worked his entire life as a draftsman at the Brooklyn Navy Yard, he devoted every hour of his spare time to documenting American railroads. Over the years his collection grew and grew. He took photographs and he collected photographs and gradually he assembled over 20,000 3-X-4-inch negatives documenting over 550 American railroads. The photographs in Chaney's collection dated from the 1840s to the 1940s and covered railroads from every corner of North America. Chaney retired in 1942 and returned to Baltimore where he died on 5 April 1948.

CB Chaney was typical of the photographers from Alexander Gardner who followed the Union Pacific west in 1864 to men like Nils Huxtable who follow the great iron horses to this day. These are the people for whom both photography and railroads are part and parcel of the cultural heritage of this continent, and it is to them that this book is fondly dedicated.

Below: *The crew of a Pennsylvania Railroad 0-6-0 switcher at the shops in Altoona. The Pennsy added a touch of elegance to the bustling, industrial village of 8000 when it built the luxurious Logan House.*

THE SOURCE

orth America's first railroads sprang up in the heavily populated northeastern United States, and upon these early lines the first important railroad empires developed. Indeed, it was in the Northeast that the first locomotives were built. As compared with the steam and diesel locomotives that became familiar in the twentieth century, those built in 1830 seem tiny and curiously designed. The first locomotives constructed for actual service weighed from three to five tons; the weight of the *DeWitt Clinton*, for example, was 3.5 tons. The English imports were double that weight and proved too heavy for the tracks with rails of wood surfaced with strap iron. The *John Bull* engine, imported in 1831 for use on the Camden & Amboy line connecting New York and Philadelphia, weighed 10 tons, and was the heaviest engine yet run in the United States. Indeed, its great size was a positive disadvantage to the company for some time.

The American locomotives and cars, unlike the English and those on the Continent (where English models were generally followed) adopted a swivel truck. After the first few years practically all American locomotives had eight wheels, four driving wheels under the rear part of the engine and a four-wheeled truck carrying the fore part of the boiler. The truck was fastened to the engine by a bolt which permitted the truck to swing or swivel through several degrees around sharp curves. The swiveling truck idea seems to have occurred to several people about the same time. Ross Winans, of Baltimore, used it under a passenger coach in 1831. Later in the same year he placed a truck under the forward part of a locomotive. Also in 1831 the truck principle was applied to two locomotives built in New York. One was designed by Horatio Allen, chief engineer of the Charleston & Hamburg Railroad, and the other by John B Jervis, chief engineer for the Mohawk & Hudson. The engine planned by Jervis was more in accordance with subsequent designs, and to him the greater credit is due.

The American, or Campbell, type locomotive had four connected driving wheels and a four-wheeled truck. The first engine of this design was built in 1836 by James Brooks for Henry R Campbell, both of Philadelphia. This rapidly became the prevailing design for the passenger service, and remained so throughout the nineteenth century.

One essential feature of the locomotive awaited introduction until 1837—the use of equalizing beams by means of which the weight on the driving wheels had a vertical motion independent of the other wheels, and could move without greatly changing the pressure imposed by the wheel on the track. Equalizing beams were first used in the *Hercules*, designed by Joseph Harrison Jr and constructed by the Baldwin Locomotive Works.

The big railroads of the northeast corridor, known as the trunk lines, came to possess the same relationship to North America that the spinal cord has to the human body. Railroads ran to the continent's extremities with single and occasionally double-tracked lines. From Philadelphia and New York to Boston, the great trunk lines were quadruple tracked. In some places, the quadruple tracks were quadrupled again. The two largest lines, between whom an intense rivalry existed, were the Pennsylvania and the New York Central. Each had more than 25,000 miles of track. The New York Central began in 1831 as the Mohawk & Hudson and grew into a rail empire of immense proportions after 1869 under the guidance of Cornelius Vanderbilt—the 'Commodore'—and his successors. The other great trunk lines included the Baltimore & Ohio, the Chesapeake & Ohio and the Erie Railroad, which were also controlled by Cornelius Vanderbilt.

Vanderbilt is a name which, in the late nineteenth-century United States, became almost synonymous with boundless wealth. This wealth was acquired, however, not by any lucky stroke of fortune, a fortunate deal at a gambling table, or the wholesale swindling so often gilded with the name of speculation, but by a combination of unflagging industry and rare perception of the fitness of means to ends—usually commendable means and ends almost invariably for the welfare of the community.

Cornelius Vanderbilt was born on Staten Island in 1794, the son of a thriving farmer, who owned his farm and carried his produce to the New York markets in his own sailboat. Cornelius was a sturdy lad, a leader in athletic feats on land and water, and a daring rider.

By 1853, the Commodore had parlayed $500 into control of a steamship line and a few years later he built the Staten Island Railroad and began withdrawing his money from steamships for railroad investments. In 1860 he bought the Harlem Railroad at below $7 a share, and a few years later he became its president when its shares were worth $30. In 1864 the same share was worth $285. This was

Facing page: This Currier and Ives print depicts the station at Hornellsville on the Erie Railway line. The locomotive on the far left is about to depart for the Western states and territories, bearing its precious cargo of mail.

the foundation of the great Vanderbilt fortune. The consolidation of the New York Central and Hudson River roads followed, and the entire system became the property of Commodore Vanderbilt.

He began at once improving the property. Useless expenditures were stopped, waste was checked, improved depots were built, tracks were relaid, and business was encouraged and developed all along the line. When Commodore Vanderbilt died on 4 January 1877, he was one of the richest men in America, his fortune amounting to more the $100 million (at least $50 billion in 1992 dollars), almost all of it in railroads.

William Henry Vanderbilt, the Commodore's eldest son, was born at the New Brunswick Hotel and was educated to run and control the New York Central and to be a railroad man. In the 1880s William H Vanderbilt acquired a substantial interest in the Reading Railroad, and there ensued a battle between the trunk lines. The shrewd head of the New York Central saw the importance of the Reading as a means of bringing the rival Pennsylvania Railroad to terms, while *also* securing for the New York Central lines the coal and coke traffic in which it was weak. The three million tons of anthracite which the Reading annually shipped to the West was desirable business for the Vanderbilt system. With the aid of William K, Reading President Franklin B Gowen again proceeded upon a program of expansion to strengthen his railroad's position in the anthracite traffic and acquire new sources and outlets for business. He revived immediately the project first broached in 1879, on the eve of receivership, to lease the Central Railroad of New Jersey for 999 years.

The new traffic connections secured by cooperation with the Vanderbilts also involved a heavy financial burden. The plan developed by Gowen and Vanderbilt involved nothing less than the transformation of the Reading from a local coal road into a system of trunk-line proportions.

Meanwhile, a syndicate headed by Vanderbilt was formed to build a new line from the Reading at Harrisburg to Pittsburgh, to be known as the South Pennsylvania Railroad Company. By holding out the promise of lower rates, aid for the project was obtained from Andrew Carnegie and other leading Pittsburgh industrialists, who charged the Pennsylvania with monopolistic practices. From Pittsburgh the new line was to reach the West over the Pittsburgh & Lake Erie, which the Vanderbilts had acquired in 1882. This railroad was to constitute virtually a western extension for the Reading.

William H Vanderbilt died in 1885, having transferred the active management of his railroads to his sons, Cornelius and William K in 1881. It was under the management of William K Vanderbilt that the New York, Chicago & St Louis, known as the 'great double track nickel-plated' road or simply as the 'Nickel Plate' Railroad, which had been built as a competing line, was purchased outright in 1883.

Right: The DeWitt Clinton *was the first locomotive built by the West Point Foundry for the Mohawk & Hudson, the first of the small lines that were later to merge into the New York Central.*

Named the Dewitt Clinton *for the prominent New Yorker who was the driving force behind the Erie Canal, the engine made its inaugural run on 9 August 1931, connecting Albany with Schenectady.*

Below: *The DeWitt Clinton of the Mohawk & Hudson was notable for the simplicity of its construction. It weighed some 6758 pounds and was 11.5 feet in length. The engine was mounted on four wheels, and the tender was nothing more than a wagon with a canopy. Behind the tender were passenger cars that resembled stage coaches.*

Right: *One of the last posters for the Mohawk & Hudson, before the name change to Albany & Schenectady.*

Right, below: *An 1852 timetable for the Buffalo & State Line Rail Road, later renamed the Lake Shore. The line ran for about 68 miles along the south shore of Lake Erie to the Pennsylvania border.*

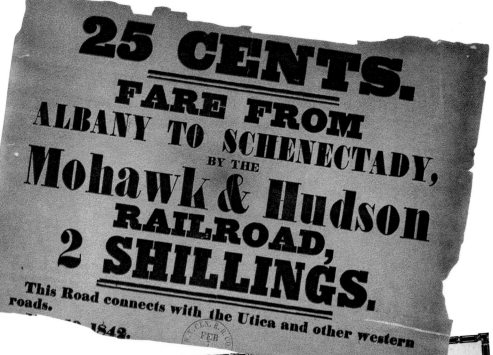

		PASSING WEST			STATIONS	PASSING EAST				
No. 1. Clevel'd Exp	No. 2. Exp Mail	No. 3. Acc'n & Fr't	No. 4. Night Exp.	No. 5. Fr'ght Tuesday, Thursday & Saturday		No. 1. Night Exp.	No. 2. Acc'n & Fr't	No. 3. Exp. Mail	No. 4. Lighting Ex	No. 5. Fr'ght Monday, Wed'day & Friday
					BUFFALO.	5 00	11 35	4 00	10 40	5 15
7 30 A. M.	10 45 A. M.	2 30 P. M.	9 30	3 00 P. M.	ROGERS' ROAD	4 31*	11 10 meet	3 44 meet	10 23*	4 45
7 50*	11 10 meet	3 00	9 50	3 44 meet	1st MILE CREEK	4 20*	10 45	3 32 meet	10 10* m't	4 20
8 00*	11 22	3 32 meet	10 10 meet	4 04	EVANS CENTRE	4 08*	10 25	3 17	10 02*	3 51 meet
8 12	11 40	3 51 meet	10 40	4 32	SAW MILL	3 56*	10 05*	3 02*	9 55*	3 15
8 17*	11 50*	4 00*	10 50*	4 44*	IRVING	3 49	9 55	3 00	9 50*	3 00 pass'd
8 22*	11 58	4 10	11 05	4 59	SILVER CREEK	3 44	9 35	2 52	9 45	2 40
8 30	12 10 P. M.	4 24	11 20	5 20	DUNKIRK	3 14	9 00 meet	2 26	9 24*	2 10
9 00 meet	12 50	5 04	12 10	6 10	SALEM	2 48*	8 38	2 05	9 12*	1 33
9 15*	1 08	5 18	12 34	6 30	CENTREVILLE	2 44*	8 30	1 57	9 00*	1 18 meet.
9 20*	1 18 meet.	5 30	12 43	6 40	WESTFIELD	2 30	8 05	1 40 meet	8 48	12 30
9 35	1 40 meet	5 50	1 08	7 20	QUINCY	2 10*	7 44	1 20	8 35*	11 40
9 50*	1 55	6 15	1 28	7 45	STATE LINE	2 00 A. M.	7 30 A. M.	1 15 P. M.	8 30 P. M.	11 30 A. M.
10 00	2 00	6 25	1 35	8 00						

BUFFALO AND STATE LINE RAIL ROAD

TIME TABLE.

NO. 9.   **NO. 9.**

FOR THE INFORMATION OF EMPLOYEES ONLY.—This Time Table is not intended as an *advertisement* of Times or Hours of any Train. The Company reserve the right to vary from any of them at their pleasure, and will not be responsible for any information herein contained.

The figures set against Buffalo, Eastward, and State Line, Westward, are the times to reach these Stations; and the other figures represent the time of leaving those Stations against which they are set.

PASSING WEST—Train No. 1 will only stop at Evans Centre, Silver Creek, Dunkirk, and Westfield.
PASSING EAST—Train No. 1 will only stop at Westfield, Dunkirk Silver Creek and Irving.
"   Train No. 4 stops only at Westfield, Dunkirk, and Silver Creek.
* Trains do not stop.

MONDAY, JUNE 20, 1852.

C. C. DENNIS, Supt.

Above: No 137, a 0-4-0 'Buffalo' switcher, and No 104—the Putnam—*(at right), a 4-4-0. Both of these Boston & Albany locomotives date back to the post-Civil War era.*

The Boston & Albany was one of many small lines that provided stiff competition for the New York Central. In 1854, Erastus Corning, president of the New York Central, proposed that the railroads serving the eastern seaboard set uniform rates. An agreement was reached, but it lasted only six months, instigating a series of rate wars.

Cornelius Vanderbilt, the patriarch of the Vanderbilt family, is the personification of the American dream. Much of his rags-to-riches saga centers around the empire of the New York Central.

After arranging the merger of the New York Central and the Hudson River railroads in 1869, Vanderbilt started construction of the grandest and most magnificent railroad depot the city of New York had ever seen. Grand Central Depot (left), as it was first called, started to go up at Fourth Avenue and 42nd Street, the site of the New York & Harlem Railroad's steam locomotive terminal.

To accommodate the new depot, Vanderbilt acquired more land between Madison and Lexington avenues up to 48th Street. Two years in construction at a cost of more than $3 million, the terminal was essentially a huge cylindrical train shed—22 feet wide, 600 feet long and 100 in height at its highest point.

Right: *Grand Central Depot as it appeared in 1883. This view shows the north end of the station from the yards, opposite 46th Street.*

Above: *A passenger train crossing the first Niagara Railway Bridge in about 1860. The years between 1850 and 1860 saw a number of short connecting railroads in the East merge into long lines under single ownership.*

Originally 11 companies owned and operated the railroads composing the line connecting Albany and Buffalo, New York, and in 1850 seven distinct companies operated between those cities. The following year they were united under one management—the New York Central. Two years later the Hudson River Railroad became a part of this system, and by 1858 five more lines were added.

Improvements to passenger coaches were as integral to the growth of the railroad industry as were advances to roadbeds and locomotives. George M Pullman, an inventor and industrialist, is the man whose name is synonymous with luxury in rail travel. As a frequent rail traveler, Pullman was forced to endure the primitive sleeping accommodations found on trains and was thus inspired to remodel a coach into a sleeping car (above). He put in two ranks of berths, with the upper berth hinged to the car's side. The sleeping car was soon followed by the buffet or hotel car, drawing room and dining cars.

Right: This parlor car, dubbed the **Maritana** was another Pullman offering. Built in 1875, the car was assigned to the Maine Central Railroad. The chairs were richly upholstered, fitted with adjustable backs and revolved on a swivel. Oil lamps provided light.

Right: *The Fast Mail train offered 24-hour mail service between New York and Chicago. A joint venture between the New York Central and the United States Post Office, the Fast Mail made its inaugural run on 14 September 1875.*

The Fast Mail was an immediate success, but less than a year after its inception Congress reduced the rates it paid to railroads for carrying the mail and the service was discontinued.

In 1877, Congress appropriated increased funds and the service resumed on the New York Central as well as on other lines.

Left: *A train of the New York & Harlem Railroad crossing a trestle close to 4th Avenue in New York. Incorporated in 1831, the New York & Harlem Railroad was, at first, primarily a horsecar system operating in Manhattan from 23d Street north to 129th Street between Third and Eighth avenues. In 1840 the charter was amended to allow the railroad to build north to Albany, and by 1844 the road had reached White Plains.*

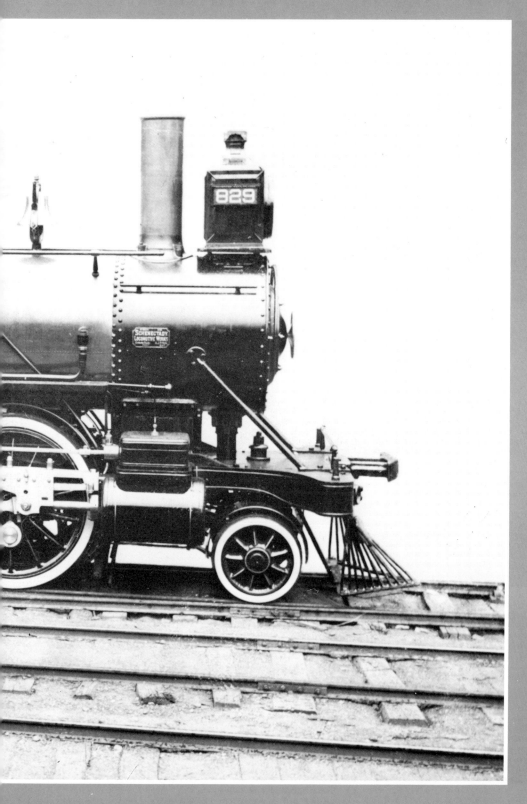

Left: *No 829 of the New York Central &
Hudson River Railroad is an excellent example of a 2-6-6 Tank-type locomotive of the late
nineteenth century. By this time, American
leadership in steam locomotion was acknowl-
edged even by British railroad pioneers.*

Above: *New York, New Haven & Hartford
trains at the yards at the Grand Central
Depot in 1889.*

Below: *The Erie Railroad used the
2-8-8-8-2 Triplex-type locomotive for heavy
freight. Locomotives of this type had three
power units (cylinders and driving wheels).
Note that the third power unit carries the
tender.*

The New York Central's famed Twentieth Century Limited *began service between New York and Chicago in 1902. The fastest, most luxurious train in the country, it made the 960-mile run to Chicago in 20 hours, for an average speed of 80 mph.*

Originally, the Century *was powered by 4-4-2 Atlantics, but in the 1920s, the Atlantics were replaced by big 4-6-4 Hudsons. Modified over the years, the most powerful version of the Hudson could attain 4700 horsepower at 75 mph. In 1938, the streamlined Hudson (these pages) was designed. The new design was essentially the same old Hudson with what one observer called 'an upside down bathtub.'*

THE INDUSTRIAL HEARTLAND

The triangle whose corners lay at Buffalo, Chicago and Washington, once contained within it an industrial power base whose might exceeded that of any nation on earth. The steel, the coal, the manufactured goods and consumer products that came forth from America's industrial heartland did so in a volume unprecedented in human history.

As these products did go forth to the world, it was aboard the rail cars of the great trunk lines of the region. Indeed it was the great trunk lines whose elaborate internal network within the region moved the raw materials and subcomponents to the manufacturers of the heartland. As we have noted, the great trunk lines came to possess the same relationship to North America that the spinal cord has to the human body. The two largest lines, the Pennsylvania Railroad and the New York Central, each had more than 25,000 miles of track, while the great Chesapeake & Ohio and the Baltimore & Ohio had nearly that much between them.

The greatest of the trunk lines, the Pennsylvania, became the largest railroad in the world, and for more than a century its lines served more of North America's industry than any other railroad. The Pennsylvania became so important that for most of the early twentieth century, it was known as the 'standard railroad of the world.'

Next in importance to the trunk lines were the railroads whose lifeblood was the transportation of coal, which was itself the lifeblood of the American economy from the middle of the nineteenth century until the middle of the twentieth. These roads were by no measure small, and many of them, such as the Philadelphia & Reading and the Delaware, Lackawanna & Western, reached trunk line proportions at one time or another.

Until 1861 the Philadelphia & Reading was little more than a link in the transportation chain whereby coal was moved from the Schuylkill coal fields into Philadelphia. However, in the 1880s as William H Vanderbilt acquired a substantial interest in the Reading, the battle between the trunk lines was particularly keen at the moment, and the shrewd head of the New York Central saw the importance of the Reading as a means of bringing the Pennsylvania Railroad to terms, while also securing for the New York Central lines the coal and coke traffic in which it was weak. The three million tons of anthracite which the Reading annually shipped to the West was desirable business for the Vanderbilt system.

With the aid of Vanderbilt, Reading President Franklin B Gowen again proceeded upon a program of expansion to strengthen his railroad's position in the anthracite traffic and acquire new sources and outlets for its business. He revived immediately the project first broached in 1879, on the eve of receivership, to lease the Central Railroad of New Jersey for 999 years.

The new traffic connections secured by cooperation with the Vanderbilts also involved a heavy financial burden. The plan developed by Gowen and Vanderbilt involved nothing less than the transformation of the Reading from a local coal road into a system of trunk-line proportions.

The Baltimore & Ohio, which was also engaged in a struggle with the Pennsylvania Railroad during the 1880s, was building a line from Baltimore to Philadelphia and negotiated a traffic agreement whereby the Philadelphia & Reading's Bound Brook route to New York was to constitute its outlet to the metropolis. The Schuylkill River East Side Railway was jointly built to connect the two systems in Philadelphia.

By the late 1870s, Jay Gould, the notorious financier, owned a group of western railroads whose eastern terminus was the Wabash at Buffalo. Gould also then virtually controlled the Central Railroad of New Jersey. This latter line, however, proved of little aid in giving him a through outlet to the Atlantic coast, and so he sought a road which would carry the Wabash business to New York. The Lackawanna, although it got no nearer Buffalo than Binghamton, seemed the most likely property, and he accumulated a substantial interest in it. By 1880, the road was commonly referred to on Wall Street as a Gould property, and in 1881 and 1882 he was on the board of directors.

Gould succeeded in getting the cooperation of the National City Bank interests in a joint venture to build a line from Binghamton to Buffalo, in order to fill the gap. In August 1880 a charter was taken out for the New York, Lackawanna & Western Railroad. This road was in turn leased to the Delaware, Lackawanna & Western in 1882 and another great New York to Buffalo trunk was born.

Facing page: *Baltimore & Ohio's Mount Clare Station, built in 1829, is the first and oldest passenger station in the United States. On 25 August 1835 the first train to enter Washington, DC left from this station.*

Left: *The* Stourbridge Lion *was brought over from England in 1828 by Horatio Allen for the Delaware & Hudson Canal Company.*

Right: *The* Tom Thumb *was the first locomotive to be built in America.*

Below: Old Ironsides, *an early locomotive of the Philadelphia, Germantown & Norristown Railroad.*

Left: *The original Atlantic, a nineteenth century B&O 'grasshopper' type locomotive, pulls a string of reproduction Imlay Coach cars at the Fair of the Iron Horse, the railroad's centennial celebration in 1927.*

Right: *In 1848, the* Pioneer *made its first run on the short Galena & Chicago Union Railroad, one of the few lines in the Midwest. Although there were 9000 miles of tracks in the US by 1850, the majority was concentrated in the Eastern States.*

In 1830, Robert L Stevens, son of shipping and horse-railroad baron John Stevens, set sail for England to buy the best locomotive he could find for his father's railroad, the Camden & Amboy of New Jersey. At the Stephenson Works, he observed the Planet *in action and ordered a copy, dubbed the* John Bull *(left) in honor of its British birthplace.*

By the end of the 1860s, railroads offered such amenities as sleeping cars, parlor cars and dining cars. The photo at left *shows the type of oil lamps that illuminated the B&O's passenger coaches in 1865.*

Left, below: An early Pullman sleeper with pull-down upper and convertible lower berths.

Right: *B&O's old No 25, the* William Mason. *Built in the 1850s, the engine is now on display at the Baltimore Railroad Museum in Baltimore.*

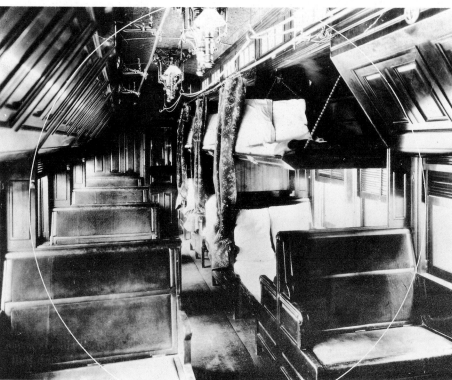

With over two-thirds of America's 30,000 miles of rails in the northern states, the Union had a decided advantage during the Civil War. Above: The B&O shops at Martinsburg, West Virginia during the war years. In 1861 Confederate General Stonewall Jackson raided the yards, destroying 42 locomotives and seizing another 14 for the Confederate forces.

Above, right: US Military Corps at work along the tracks of the Orange & Alexandria Railroad at Devereaux near Bull Run, circa 1863. The engine (at right) was named for Herman Haupt, the former general manager of the Pennsylvania Railroad, who Lincoln appointed the first chief of Military Railway Service.

Facing page: The funeral train that carried the body of the assassinated President Lincoln.

Left: The Ada Number 14, built by Baldwin, operated on the Detroit & Milwaukee Railway between Detroit and Grand Haven, Michigan in the 1870s. The Detroit & Milwaukee Railway was formed in 1855 with the merger of the Detroit & Pontiac (1838) and the Oakland & Ottawa Railroad (1848) extended its track to Grand Haven on Lake Michigan in 1858. The D&M became a part of the Grand Trunk system in the 1880s and officially a part of Grand Trunk Western on 9 May 1928, when the GTW was incorporated with the consolidation of 10 railroads.

The Delaware, Lackawanna & Western was one of lines that grew up in the rich industrial heartland of the northeast. In addition to transporting coal, the DL&W also carried passengers in coaches (left, below) supplied by the Pullman Company.

Right: The Pennsylvania Railroad's Harrisburg Station, as it appeared in the 1870s. By this time, the Pennsy had expanded from its original Philadelphia to Pittsburgh route and was a sprawling system with 6000 miles of trackage.

Camel-class locomotives were powerful engines designed to pull heavy coal-laden trains through difficult mountain terrain. Left: *No 196 of the Philadelphia & Reading Railroad carried coal from the Schuylkill coal fields to Philadelphia, while Lehigh Valley No 2006* (right) *moved coal from Mauch Chunk to Easton, Pennsylvania.*

Below: *No 213 from the Rogers Locomotive Works was the first engine to operate on the Illinois Central's suburban routes in 1880.*

Right, below: *Cornwall Railroad's* Penryn, *a 4-4-0 American type.*

Right: *This November 1896 photo shows the Baldwin Locomotive Works in Philadelphia, as viewed from the corner of 17th Street and Pennsylvania Avenue. This factory produced most of North America's steam locomotive power in the nineteenth and twentieth centuries.*

Matthias Baldwin himself (inset) started out as a watchmaker, but became the single most important locomotive builder in the United States.

Above: *NC&StL No 290, a Baldwin-built Pacific 4-6-2.*

Below: *A locomotive bearing the Baldwin Locomotive Works inscription on its tender leads a string of newly manufactured switchers.*

The Grand Trunk Western was the largest of three Canadian-owned railroads that operated in the United States. The GTW served the north central region of the United States, concentrating on the area's large industrial cities—Chicago, Detroit, Toledo and Milwaukee.

GTW No 2109 (left) was built by Baldwin in 1873 but came to an ignoble end in 1915, when it was scrapped.

Right: *This 1912 photo shows the Grand Trunk roundhouse in Durand, Michigan under construction.*

Right: *The crew of Michigan Central No 245 pose with their 4-4-0 engine in 1889. The 4-4-0, or American type, engine was the most widely used type of locomotive in nineteenth-century North America. The undisputed master of the rails until the 1880s, by 1900 the 4-4-0 was considered obsolete. However, it continued to be built in small numbers until the advent of the diesel engine in the 1940s.*

Above: The Pennsylvania Limited *crosses the Rockville bridge. The* Pennsylvania Limited *began service in 1881, running between Jersey City and Chicago in a record-breaking 26 hours and 20 minutes. Famous for its punctuality, the* Limited *was also known for its lush appointments and excellent service.*

Left: The Pennsylvania Railroad's Broad Street Station in Philadelphia.

Right: Pennsy No 420, another locomotive of the American type wheel configuration.

Left: *Reliving the past—two vintage steam locomotives lead a passenger train on a 1983 museum exhibition run through the bucolic Pennsylvania countryside.*

Above: *Pennsy No 1223, adorned with the* Pennsylvania Special *headboard. The successor to the* Pennsylvania Limited, *the* Pennsylvania Special *made its first run on 15 June 1902, making the New York-Chicago run in 20 hours. The route was discontinued in less than a year, only to re-emerge in 1905 with a new, even faster 18-hour schedule.*

Below: *Samuel Vauclain, President of the Baldwin Locomotive works, poses with his family and one of his creations—a huge 2-6-6-2 locomotive built for the B&O in the 1920s.*

In the 1940s, railroads began exploring alternate modes of motive power. The Pennsylvania Railroad, for example, harnessed steam power in a new way—the steam turbine (left). Turbine blades, not pistons, turned the wheels.

Right: *Illinois Central Railroad No 2411 at the Chicago World's Fair of 1934. This 4-8-2 locomotive was built by ALCO-Schenectady in 1923.*

The largest train station in the world, Pennsylvania Station in New York City encompassed six city blocks, between Seventh and Eighth avenues and 31st and 33d streets. This grand edifice was completed in 1910. The main waiting room (left) was modeled after the Roman Baths at Caracalla. The ceiling height soared to 150 feet, and the huge lunette windows spanned 65 feet at the base.

Right: *The Main Concourse, capped by a dome of glass and steel, was the site of countless farewells and homecomings. The wrought iron stairways led down to the track platforms, where conductors summoned passengers to the waiting cars.*

Far right: *The immense and classically designed New Savarin Restaurant at Pennsy Station was a far cry from the typical lunch counter.*

Left: *A Pennsy tunnel digging crew, led by
the chief engineer, celebrates the successful
completion of the South Tunnel under the
Hudson River on 9 October 1906. Pennsy
officials had recognized that the railroad
must have a station in New York City, which
had supplanted Philadelphia as the nation's
hub, and tunnels under the river—rather
than bridges over it—were the best way to
reach the city.*

Left: *The Pennsy's T1 Class locomotives could haul the heaviest passenger trains at over 100 mph.*

Right: *The C&O 500, a steam turbine electric locomotive. Instead of using coal and water to produce steam that turned the wheels, the steam generated electricity to run the electric motors mounted on the axles. When it was built in 1947, the 500 was longest—154 feet—passenger locomotive in the world.*

Right, below: *St Louis-San Francisco Railway's famous passenger train, the* Firefly, *one of the great streamliners of its era.*

Left: *Loaded down with Kentucky coal, C&O T-1 No 3023 emerges from the massive girders of the Limeville Bridge, heading north to Lake Erie to fire the forges of war.*

Right: *Locomotives like this B&O 0-8-0 also contributed to the war effort. The railroads' assistance during World War II extended overseas as well. Representatives from 28 railroads banded together to form the 708th Railway Grand Division. The division restored order to the European railways, transporting troops and supplies to the front.*

Below: *The heart of power—the driving wheels on a Pennsy 2-8-2.*

Above: *Heading a coal train, C&O K4 No 2716 curls around the Big Sandy Subdivsion near Prestonsburg, Kentucky in 1950.*

Right: *B&O EM-1 class No 7623. The engine was built in 1945, renumbered No 673 in 1957 and retired in 1960.*

Far right: *The Mammoths meet at Parsons Yard, Columbus, Ohio. Two C&O T1s eyeball each other under the signal bridge in 1944. This unusual perspective gives us a real appreciation for the size of these locomotives.*

THE LAND OF DIXIE

The first railroad in the United States to provide a regular steam train service was located in the South—the South Carolina Canal & Railroad Company, which made its inaugural run on 25 December 1830. By the time of the Civil War, however, the South had lost its edge in railroading. At the outset of the war, the South had just 9000 miles of track, in contrast to the 22,000 miles of track that could be found in the industrial North. This difference would play a crucial role in the outcome of the war. The North's advantage included ownership of foundries and locomotive factories, and the North had dozens scattered well away from the fighting, while the South had just one, in Richmond, Virginia.

Many of the South's railroads were caught in the thick of the fighting. In one famous incident, Union soldiers stole a Western & Atlantic locomotive named *The General*. A dramatic chase ensued, with Confederate soldiers retaking the locomotive. In 1861 the Confederates won one of their greatest Civil War battles when they eluded Union forces assigned to watch them and rode the Manassas Gap Railroad across the Blue Ridge Mountains to Bull Run, which turned the tide in their favor.

Of course, the railroads of the South were also the target of destruction. Union soldiers stoked the fireboxes of Confederate locomotives without water to make them explode. Then they tore rails from the tracks, heated them up and twisted them around trees so they could not be reused by southern forces. The twisted rails were known as 'Sherman's neckties.'

After the war, the South's network of rails was substantially reconstructed. Some roads, like the West Point Route, never recovered financially; others, such as the Norfolk & Western, prospered.

The Norfolk & Western can trace its roots to the Norfolk & Petersburg, which was chartered in 1850 to build a line between those two Virginia cities. By 1858, the Norfolk & Petersburg had reached Petersburg, having crossed an area known as the Dismal Swamp on tracks laid on a mat of trees and logs. In 1867 the Norfolk & Petersburg consolidated with two other railroads: the Southside Railroad, which operated between Petersburg and Lynchburg, Tennessee, and the Virginia & Tennessee, which operated between Lynchburg and Bristol, Tennessee. Thus, a line was created, extending from the Atlantic coast to halfway across Tennessee. Three years later, in 1870, the three railroads merged to become the Atlantic, Mississippi & Ohio.

In 1881, the Clark banking interests of Philadelphia acquired the AM&O and renamed it the Norfolk & Western. As was happening with railroads all over the United States, the next 30 years was a time of rapid expansion for the Norfolk & Western, which extended north to Columbus and Cincinnati, Ohio, and south to North Carolina. Like the Reading Railroad to the north, the Norfolk & Western found its livelihood in hauling coal. In fact, thanks to an abundance of coal in its territory, the Norfolk & Western resisted dieselization until the late 1950s.

In 1959, the Norfolk & Western merged with the Virginian Railroad in the first of a series of mergers and acquisitions that resulted in the Norfolk & Western of today. The Atlantic & Danville was bought in 1962. The big merger year was 1964, when the Wabash, the Akron, Canton, & Youngstown, and the New York, Chicago & St Louis—the Nickel Plate Road—were absorbed. The latter acquisition also brought the Wheeling & Lake Erie, which had previously merged with the Nickel Plate. As a result of these acquisitions, the Norfolk & Western today operates in 14 states and one Canadian province, from Norfolk, Virginia and Buffalo, New York in the East, and westward to Kansas City, St Louis and Omaha. The industrial areas of Pittsburgh, Cleveland, Cincinnati, Indianapolis and Detroit are served, as well as the coal fields of West Virginia, Kentucky and Ohio.

In 1982, the Norfolk Southern Corporation was formed as a holding company to effect the merger of the Norfolk & Western with the Southern Railway System. Although each line continues to operate independently, several terminal operations have been consolidated.

The earliest precursor of the Southern Railway was the South Carolina Canal & Railroad Company. Chartered in 1828, just a year after the Baltimore & Ohio, the South Carolina Canal & Railroad Company can claim the distinction of being one of the oldest railroads in North America, and although it was not the first railroad to offer regular service, it was the first to provide a regular *steam* train. When the 136-mile line between Charleston and Hamburg, South Carolina was completed, the South Carolina Canal & Railroad was the longest in the world.

The railroad was initially established to secure cotton traffic for the port city of Savannah, Georgia. It also provided a passenger service that covered the first 90-mile stretch from the coast in ten and a half hours. Passengers then spent the night at somewhat crude accommodations before continuing the trip the next morning. Locomotive headlamps soon made traveling by night possible.

Facing page: A Currier & Ives portrayal of life along the Mississippi—a steam locomotive racing a riverboat.

In time, the South Carolina Canal & Railroad merged with a number of small southern lines, such as the Richmond & Danville and the East Tennessee, Virginia & Georgia, forming a network that became the Southern Railway in 1894.

Well into the twentieth century, the Southern continued to grow, acquiring more railroads until it ruled the South. One of its major acquisitions was Central of Georgia in 1963. In 1974, Southern Railway acquired the Norfolk Southern, which was itself a road with a long and varied history, dating back to 1870 when it was chartered as the Elizabeth City & Norfolk Railroad. Construction began on this railroad in 1880, with a line from Berkley, Virginia (now Norfolk) along the Dismal Swamp to Elizabeth City, North Carolina. By 1881, the railroad had reached Edenton, along the Albemarle Sound, where steamships connected with the trains for points up the various rivers and along the North Carolina coast.

In 1883, the Elizabeth City & Norfolk was renamed the Norfolk Southern. By the end of the decade, the Norfolk & Southern had entered receivership and was reorganized as the Norfolk & Southern Railroad in 1891.

The next thirty years saw expansion as well as financial struggle. In 1906 the Norfolk & Southern Railroad consolidated with the Virginia & Carolina Coast Railroad, the Raleigh & Pamlico Sound Railroad, the Pamlico, Oriental & Western Railway and the Beaufort & Western Railroad to form the Norfolk & Southern Railway. The new N&S also held the lease of the Atlantic & North Carolina. However, the cost of expansion was more than the railroad could bear and it was again placed in receivership in 1908.

The expansion program continued, but the Depression drove the Norfolk Southern into receivership yet again, and throughout the 1930s the railroad sold off some of its smaller lines. In 1947 the company was taken over by a group of investors headed by Patrick B McGinnis. Under his direction, the railroad acquired a pair of office cars, leased apartments or hotel suites in New York, Washington and Miami, lavishly entertained its shippers and ended up being investigated by the ICC. McGinnis resigned and new management took over in 1953.

In 1974, the Norfolk Southern was acquired by Southern Railway and merged with the Carolina & Northwestern under the Norfolk Southern name. However, in 1981 the name was changed to Carolina & Northwestern so that the Norfolk Southern name could be used for the holding company formed by the merger of the Southern Railway with the Norfolk & Western. In 1985, Norfolk Southern purchased Conrail, making Southern Railway part of the largest railroad system in the United States.

Right: *The wood-burning* Best Friend of Charleston *was the first locomotive built in America for regular service on a railroad. Service was inaugurated on Christmas Day 1830, when the* Best Friend *puffed away from Charleston, South Carolina over a railroad that is now part of the Southern Railway system.*

During the Civil War, 18 Union soldiers, assisted by two civilians, operating under cover in Shanty, Georgia stole The General (these pages), a Western & Atlantic locomotive, and headed North. Their plan was to burn railroad bridges, thus crippling the Confederate forces' ability to move supplies between Atlanta and the front at Chat-tanooga, Tennessee. The General's conductor gave chase, along with the engineer and a W&A foreman—first on foot, then a push car and finally on commandeered locomotives. Their dogged pursuit prevented the raiders from doing serious damage and they finally abandoned The General just beyond Ring-gold, Georgia.

The first railroad in Texas opened on 1 August 1853 at Harrisburg, with the locomotives General Sherman *and* Texas *(left). In 1862, the* Texas *was involved in a dramatic chase, as Confederate soldiers on the* Texas *pursued Union soldiers who had stolen* The General, *a Western & Atlantic locomotive (see page 66).*

Right, above: *A train of the United States Military Railroad crosses a troop-guarded bridge on the Orange & Alexandria Railroad, sometime during the Civil War.*

Right: *The Orange & Alexandria roundhouse and depot as it appeared in 1863. The O&A later became part of the Southern Railway System.*

Central of Georgia was the first railroad to operate in the state when The Florida, *an American type 4-4-0, hauled a passenger train from Madison to Atlanta.*

The Georgia prospered in the days before the Civil War, but suffered greatly at the hands of Union General William T Sherman during his infamous March to the Sea. After the war, the Georgia acquired the Atlanta & West Point Railroad and became co-owner of the Western Railway of Alabama. In 1881, the three lines were leased to Colonel William M Wadley.

The locomotives pictured on this page date back to the era when Wadley assumed control of the Georgia. No 146 (right) is a 4-6-0 built by Baldwin in 1884; No 1559 (right, below) was built in 1888.

Facing page, top: *Mississippi Central No 101, a 4-4-0, circa 1900.*

Facing page, bottom: *This 4-6-0 locomotive was built by Rogers Locomotive Company in 1897 for the Mobile & Ohio Railroad.*

ROGERS LOCOMOTIVE COMPANY,
PATERSON, NEW JERSEY - UNITED STATES OF AMERICA.

Below: *This Baldwin-built 4-8-4 once charged up and down the eastern seaboard during the heyday of the Atlantic Coast line.*

Right: *This Pacific-type locomotive began life on the Florida East Coast Railway. In 1935, No 750 was purchased by the Savannah & Atlanta, and remained with that line until its retirement in 1962, when it was given to the Atlanta Chapter of the National Railway Historical Society.*

The Savannah & Atlanta became part of the Southern Railway System when it was acquired by the Central of Georgia, a subsidiary of the Southern, now part of Norfolk Southern. Today, No 750 is a regular participant in Norfolk Southern's annual program of steam-powered excursion trains.

Right: *Rail enthusiast C Norman Beasley took this photograph of a Louisville & Nashville steam locomotive as it hauled a 100-car coal train through the Kentucky countryside on a warm September afternoon in 1955, one hundred years after the first L&N train made its first run.*

Once known as 'the railroad that carried coal,' the L&N was one of the last holdouts against the diesel locomotive because of its access to cheap bituminous coal in Kentucky and Tennessee. The railroad did not buy its first diesels for freight until 1950 and did not become fully dieselized until 1957, when it scrapped its last 36 steam locomotives.

Left: *An impressive view of the driving mechanism of a high speed Class A Norfolk & Western locomotive.*

In 1982, Norfolk & Western merged with the Southern Railway to form the Norfolk Southern Corporation.

These pages: *Norfolk & Western's J-611 was recovered from the Roanoke Transportation Museum and restored in Southern Railway's Birmingham, Alabama steam shops. The 'J' is the last survivor of the streamlined steam locomotives built in N&W shops around 1950. Today, J-611 pulls steam excursions.*

THE SOUTHWEST AND THE SANTA FE

Before Mexico received its independence from Spain, Santa Fe existed as an exotic city nestling in the remoteness of the 'Great American Desert.' Between Santa Fe and the United States lay some 800 miles of faintly marked trail, snaking its ways across the plains and through the mountains. This barely visible thoroughfare was destined to become a major artery of commerce. Traders from United States outposts to the east were met with a notable lack of enthusiasm upon arrival at Santa Fe. The ruling Spaniards discouraged trade by the simple and excellent expedient of jailing unsuspecting traders and confiscating their merchandise.

The first successful attempt to carry on overland trade with Santa Fe was a small expedition from Missouri organized and led by Captain William Becknell in 1821, shortly after Mexico gained its freedom. So successful was Becknell's first trip that a larger expedition was formed the next year and a new and shorter route to Santa Fe was pioneered and mapped.

Both routes—known collectively as the Santa Fe Trail—departed southwesterly from Council Grove, Kansas, and intersected the Arkansas River near Great Bend, following the river to a point just east of Dodge City. Here the trails diverged, one branch heading generally south and west across the plains to Las Vegas, and the other, more generally used, followed the Arkansas River to La Junta and turned south over the Raton Pass to Las Vegas.

Both of these routes are roughly the same as those followed by the Santa Fe Railroad of today. After Becknell's second caravan, commerce over the Santa Fe Trail expanded by leaps and bounds. Today, the mere mention of Santa Fe is sufficient to conjure up images of that railroad: bright red and yellow diesels followed by gleaming stainless steel passenger coaches and long freight trains thundering across the plains through waving wheat fields.

The charter for the Atchison & Topeka Railroad—the base from which its present system grew—was prepared single-handedly by young Cyrus Holliday in a hotel room in Lawrence, Kansas in 1859. As a member of the Territorial Legislature, Holliday introduced the charter on 1 February 1859. With the skids greased by his foresight and advance groundwork, the bill sailed through both the House and Senate and was approved by the Governor on February 11.

The Civil War and the disarranged business conditions of the country made the raising of investment capital a lengthy and heartbreaking task, a struggle that endured for 10 years. Nevertheless, the company was organized in 1860, in the Atchison office of Luther Challis.

On 3 March 1863 a territorial law setting aside 2,931,247.54 acres for the company, dependent on construction of a railroad was passed, but it was not until 30 October 1868 that Holliday saw the real beginning of the railroad—the turning of the first spade of earth at Topeka, near the bank of the Kaw River. The first construction was a pile bridge across the Kaw River, connecting the Kansas Pacific Railroad. Holliday took the occasion of the ground breaking to forecast again that the line would eventually extend to the city of Santa Fe. Carried away by his own enthusiasm and the festive note of the occasion, he confidently predicted the road would, in time, reach the Pacific and the Gulf of Mexico. At the time, people thought he was crazy, but eventually his prediction would be borne out.

The Atchison, Topeka & Santa Fe—known simply as the Santa Fe—reached the Kansas-Colorado border in 1872—one year ahead of the 10-year deadline set by Congress to claim title to the land grants. Continued progress also set the stage for a showdown with another competitor, the Denver & Rio Grande Railroad, which had expansion plans of its own in Colorado.

William Jackson Palmer, who had been a Union calvary general in the Civil War, organized the Denver & Rio Grande in 1870 to build southward from Denver to El Paso and then on to Mexico City, as much as the Santa Fe wanted to reach Pueblo and Canyon City, already served by the Denver & Rio Grande.

By this time, Boston financiers Thomas and Joseph Nickerson had wrested control of the Santa Fe from Holliday (although he stayed on as secretary of the board of directors). These two brothers recognized the need to expand the business of the railroad beyond carrying cattle and buffalo hides. They wanted to generate revenue from the various types of mining opportunities available in the Rocky Mountains of Colorado.

Palmer did not want to build a railroad competing against the Santa Fe, so he traveled East to persuade the new owners of the Santa Fe to cooperate in building one line. But his mission failed, setting up a confrontation for control of two important mountain passes—Raton Pass from Colorado and the Royal Gorge in southern Colorado.

The first clash came in early 1873. Legal rights to the 8000-foot Raton Pass, located 15 miles south of Trinidad, Colorado, were ambiguous. Both railroads

Facing page: A Santa Fe 10-wheeler hauls the first of the famed California Limiteds into Los Angeles.

claimed title, although Thomas Nickerson did not believe that the line would support a rail service. But Holliday convinced Nickerson and others on the Santa Fe board of directors of the need to expand into New Mexico.

The showdown came at Pueblo, where Rio Grande crews were met by Bat Masterson, the famous Dodge City marshall. Masterson, who boasted a long list of legally justified killings, had just been imported to protect the Santa Fe's property. He had with him a gang of armed men to keep the property safe from Rio Grande employees.

As the Rio Grande train approached, loaded with armed men, Masterson ordered his gang to surround the roundhouse where the train would stop at Pueblo, and told them to prepare to shoot. But no shots were fired. When the Rio Grande boys saw Masterson and his men with their revolvers, carbines and shotguns drawn, the threat was more than enough to stop a fight.

Under a white flag of truce, leaders from the two armed camps discussed the issue. The Rio Grande forces decided to buy off Masterson, thus retaking the Pueblo roundhouse without violence. Masterson and his men, being in this case complete mercenaries, readily complied. Their pockets now jingling with more money, the contented Masterson and his merry men laid down their arms and left peaceably under the protection of law officers.

The war was not yet over. The dispatcher's office remained in the hands of Santa Fe men, who were not about to give ground. When Rio Grande men assaulted the office with a barrage of bullets, two men were killed and two were injured.

Finally the two sides, tired of the ensuing guerilla warfare, came to a conference table in Boston in February 1880. Santa Fe voluntarily gave up its lease with Rio Grande and the rights to the Royal Gorge Canyon. In essence, the Santa Fe was allowed to continue its transcontinental conquest while the Denver & Rio Grande was allowed to expand locally in Colorado.

The first Santa Fe train to the namesake city arrived 16 February 1880. Albuquerque was reached 15 April 1880 and six months later tracks were laid as far south as San Marcial without any sign of stopping. A connection at Deming, with another road building east from California, on 8 March 1881, gave the nation its second transcontinental line.

By 1888 the Santa Fe had acquired both the St Louis & San Francisco (the 'Frisco') and the Chicago, Cincinnati & St Louis Railway, which included track between Chicago and the West Coast to the Gulf of Mexico.

From the turning of the first spade of Kansas earth on 30 October 1868, the little railroad had within a span of 20 years become one of the greatest systems in the world—a railroad that extended from the shores of Lake Michigan to the Pacific Coast and the Gulf of Mexico. The dream of Cyrus K Holliday had been fulfilled.

Right: While en route West, the passengers on board a Santa Fe train might enjoy a spontaneous race against a Wells Fargo stagecoach.

Left: A vintage Santa Fe locomotive and passenger train cross the Canyon Diablo Bridge in Arizona.

Right: *No 5-0—the* Thomas Sherlock— *was built for Sante Fe by the Taunton Locomotive works in 1870. It weighed 30.5 tons and had four drive wheels, each 67.5 inches in diameter.*

Left: *An early Santa Fe passenger train pulls into the dusty station in El Paso, Texas, not far from the border with New Mexico. Within a short time service would be extended into New Mexico and the cities of Santa Fe and Albuquerque.*

By 16 February 1880, the Santa Fe had reached its namesake city, and by mid-April it had reached Albuquerque. It began to seem that the dream of reaching the Pacific was not so far-fetched after all. Indeed, the nation's second transcontinental railroad was completed on 8 March 1881, when the Santa Fe met another road building east from California at Deming, New Mexico.

Above: *A wood-burning 4-4-0 American type locomotive named* Stowe *at the El Paso roundhouse. The locomotive belonged to the Texas & New Orleans Railroad, a subsidiary of the Southern Pacific.*

Left: *No 1, the first locomotive owned by the El Paso & Southwestern, one of the earliest railroads to cross the deserts of the old Southwest.*

On 9 July 1905, the Coyote Special, a Santa Fe train chartered by Walter Scott charged out of Los Angeles. Its destination: Chicago, in only 46 hours. The Coyote Special came to a stop at Chicago's Dearborn Station 44 hours and 54 minutes later, besting the fastest previous run by eight hours.

The train at left is a replica of the Coyote Special and was made for a television special celebrating the fiftieth anniversary of the 'Death Valley Scotty's' famous run. Locomotive No 1010 was one of the engines used in this record run and today is on display at the California State Railroad Museum in Sacramento, California.

Right: Bell clanging loudly, this long Santa Fe passenger train nears a grade crossing. The poles and wires that line the tracks, like the Santa Fe itself, were emblems of westward expansion.

Below: The Santa Fe station and Harvey House at Amarillo, Texas.

Above: *Southern Pacific's coal-burning locomotive No 3301 near El Paso, Texas. Southern Pacific experimented with oil as a fuel as early as 1879 and by 1895 oil had replaced coal on some lines.*

Right: *A few of the locals outside Southern Pacific's Phoenix, Arizona station in 1907.*

Below: *The Southern Pacific Station in Beaumont, Texas, near the Louisiana border. The line between New Orleans and Los Angeles, the Sunset Route, started operating on 12 January 1883, although Beaumont had been an important rail head for years.*

Overleaf: *A Southern Pacific freight train, headed by No 3312, crosses a bridge near Santa Rosa, New Mexico. Southern Pacific extended its line into New Mexico with the acquisition of the El Paso & Southwestern in 1924.*

It is often said that Fred Harvey (right) civilized the West. Harvey, a low-key, refined Englishman, made the Santa Fe Railroad famous for the restaurants along its routes. Before Harvey came along, passengers had to endure horrible meals at dingy railroad depots. In cooperation with the Santa Fe, Harvey offered passengers excellent food in fine surroundings, and soon numerous Harvey Houses sprang up along the Santa Fe.

Fine food was only part of the Fred Harvey story. Service was equally important, so Harvey recruited young women to work in his restaurants. Many of the young women, who came to be called 'Harvey Girls' (above), ended up marrying Santa Fe conductors or engineers, or the local ranchers or farmers.

Left: *The lunchroom at Fred Harvey's LaPosada Hotel in Winslow, Arizona, in the 1920s.*

Right: *Building the behemoth—the Southern Pacific erecting shop at Sparks, Nevada, in 1944.*

Facing page: *SP No 3808 on an electric hoist in El Paso.*

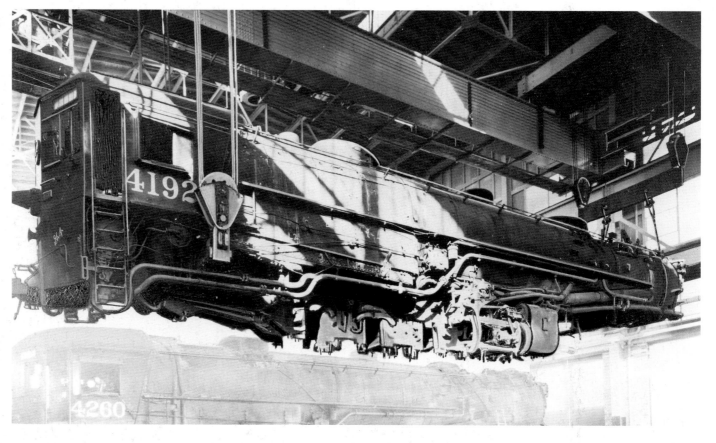

Below: *The Texas & New Orleans round-house in Houston, looking west from Harvey Street before the 1920 fire.*

Below: *This 1925 photo shows the* Golden State Limited *on its 61-hour run between Chicago and Los Angeles. One of the finest and fastest luxury trains of its day, the* Golden State Limited *offered club and observation cars, barber shops, showers and baths, and maid and valet service.*

Right: *Conductor James Cardwell and Engineer John Farley of the Southern Pacific take a moment to discuss the day's schedule.*

For nearly a century, the Santa Fe was renowned for the comfort, luxury and speed it offered its passengers. Aboard the Santa Fe, passengers could have it all—a cool drink in a comfortable club car (left) or a breath of fresh air and a bird's eye view of the rugged terrain (right).

Below: *Santa Fe No 3709 winds its way through the rocky foothills of the West.*

INFORMATION

TICKETS

Three interior views of Southern Pacific's Houston Station in 1934: the waiting room (left); the ticket counter, attended by three serious agents (above); and the dining room (right).

Left: *A Santa Fe stock car from the mid-1950s and a refrigerator car, aka a 'reefer' (left, below), from the late 1940s. Note the open ice hatches on the top.*

Right: *An eastbound Santa Fe Grand Canyon running around a freight train in Cajon Pass, where the main line crosses the coast range of mountains.*

The history of the Santa Fe's motive power is shown below, left to right—from early steam to modern diesel. The passage of time would write yet another chapter as the powerful engines seen here were replaced with advanced diesel road switchers with modular electronic components.

Right: Two Santa Fe 2-10-2s assist El Capitan's diesel unit up the steep grade of Raton Pass, just below Wooten, Colorado.

Right, below: Some of the 30,000 railfans who visited the Chicago Exposition of 1938 to marvel at Santa Fe's finest diesel and steam engines. The Blue Goose, *the second engine from the left, represents the state-of-the-art in steam motive power.*

THE AMERICAN DREAM

On 1 July 1862, President Abraham Lincoln signed the Pacific Railroad Act. Its purpose was two-fold. First, it called for the long-held dream of a railroad to span the continent and bind the nation with a band of steel at a time when it was being torn apart by Civil War. The Act also had the effect of creating the Union Pacific Railroad Company to build a line westward from Omaha, Nebraska. It also authorized the Central Pacific to 'start at or near San Francisco or some point on the navigable waters of the Sacramento River and build eastwardly to the western boundary of California, and…continue construction until meeting the line of the Union Pacific.'

Although no meeting point was specified, both railroads wanted to reach Salt Lake City first. The question of where they would meet was one of speed, until Congress stepped in on 10 April 1869 to dictate the 'the common terminal of the Union Pacific and the Central Pacific shall be at or near Ogden, Utah.'

Construction of the Union Pacific finally got underway on 5 November 1865, nearly three years behind the Central Pacific, but the work was moving considerably faster. Laying tracks across wonderfully flat expanses of Nebraska prairie bore no similarity to the difficulties encountered in the Sierra.

Because the Union Pacific was, in a sense, America's 'national' railroad, it received a great deal of attention from photographers wishing to record this historic enterprise for posterity. Alexander Gardner followed the construction of the road's Eastern Division from the Missouri River to Hays City, Kansas and accompanied Union Pacific surveyors as they moved ahead of the track laying crews. While the Central Pacific had its sights set on completing its line east across Nevada and part of Utah to Salt Lake, Union Pacific surveyors had laid out a route westward all the way to the California border.

The Central Pacific, meanwhile, continued to drive eastward. Its Chinese laborers—initially recruited when new silver mines lured other workers—had learned quickly, pushing rails eastward through the mountains and across the Nevada desert to Utah's western border by 1869. When Charles Crocker, CP's construction boss, heard that the Union Pacific crews had topped his previous record by laying eight miles of track in one day, he bet $10,000 on the ability of his own crews. The Chinese workers, he said, could lay 10 miles of rail 'between daylight and dark.' After careful planning, his crews swung into action, laying 10 miles and 56 feet in less than 12 hours.

Finally, on 10 May 1869, Central Pacific and Union Pacific locomotives sat a shoveltoss of coal apart at Promontory, Utah, just north of the Great Salt Lake.

Plans for the heroic joining had been laid well ahead of time and photographers such as Captain Andrew Joseph Russell, Charles R Savage and Alfred A Hart were on hand to record the historic moment in photographs that would be widely reproduced in publications from *Harper's Weekly* to *The Police Gazette*. The Central Pacific president and former Governor of California, Leland Stanford, would join the Union Pacific Vice President Thomas Durant in driving home a final gold spike with a silver sledge hammer.

It had taken more than half a century from the time the nation's first railroad was chartered to build a transcontinental railroad. It took only 12 more years to build the second, this one coming to a junction in New Mexico and providing the first direct line to southern California. Two years later, St Paul was linked to the Pacific Northwest, and New Orleans got a connection to the West Coast.

The system grew rapidly after that. Five more years saw the completion of a southern route between Chicago and California. The Atchison, Topeka & Santa Fe met the Southern Pacific in 1881, and finished its own route to the coast across New Mexico and Arizona in 1883.

Meanwhile, the Denver, Rio Grande & Western became the defacto 'trunk line' of the Colorado, Utah and New Mexico region. Founded in 1870, the railroad built a vast and intricate network throughout the ore-rich mining country of the Rockies of Colorado and the adjacent states. One of the America's smaller roads, the Denver Rio Grande & Western remains in service to this day as both a freight and passenger road—one of the last.

Facing page: *The men who built the Union Pacific Railroad. They numbered 10,000 strong by the time the railroad was completed in 1869. About one in four were tracklayers; the rest were graders, teamsters, herdsmen, cooks, bakers, blacksmiths, bridge-builders, carpenters, masons and clerks. Many were Irish and most were veterans of the Civil War.*

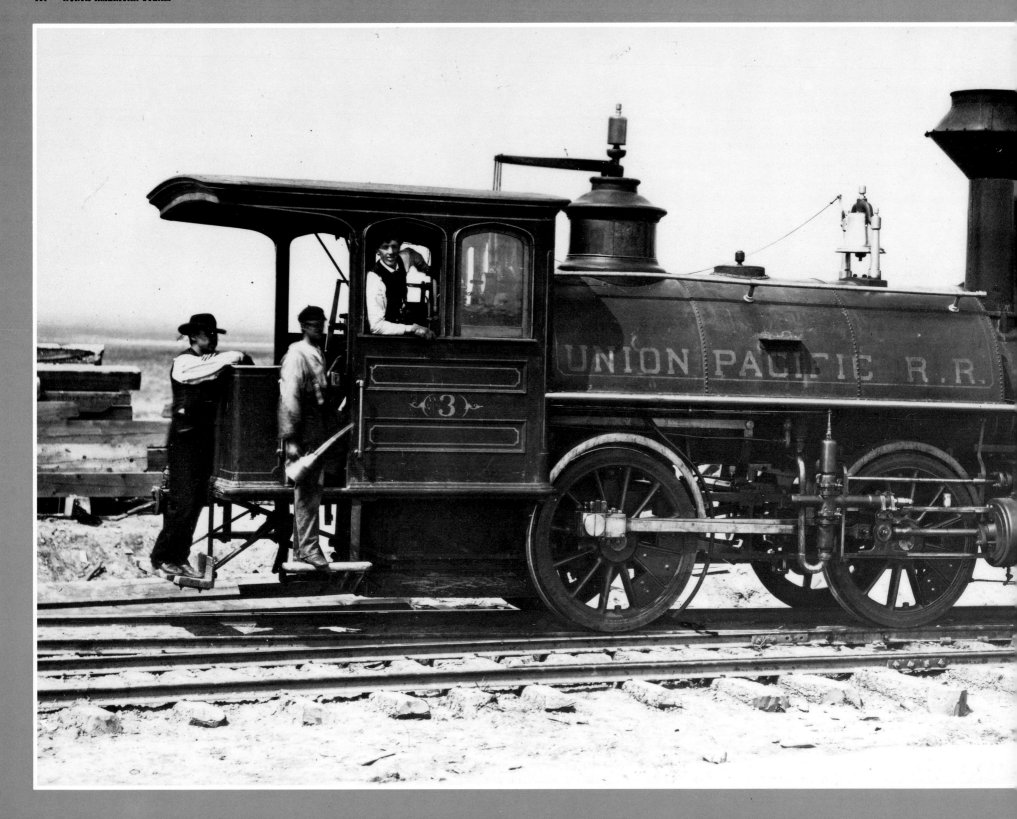

Left: *An early 'Pony' steam locomotive used during the building of the Union Pacific Railroad, the nation's first transcontinental railroad.*

Above: *The steamboats* Denver *and* Colorado *unload materials on the banks of the Missouri River at Omaha, Nebraska for construction of the Union Pacific.*

Right: *Samuel B Reed, general superintendent and engineer of construction, regards the progress made thus far on the Union Pacific.*

Right: *Construction workers, nicknamed 'Irish Terriers,' confront some of the most difficult grading in the building of the UP. Successive shelves were hacked into the rock, then pick-axed and blasted down to grade. Rough temporary tracks were laid to haul rubble away. On the higher levels, two-wheeled mule carts and wheelbarrows did the job.*

Right: *The* General Sherman *was the first locomotive purchased by the Union Pacific. It was delivered by boat from St Louis in 1865.*

Left: *A Union Pacific woodburner pauses by the water tank at the Green River Bridge in Wyoming. Snow-covered Citadel Rock is prominent in the background.*

Left: *From the West Coast, the Central Pacific forged ahead to meet the Union Pacific. This photo of an engine and a water car was taken during construction in 1868 at Winnemucca, Nevada, 325 miles east of Sacramento. Water was a precious commodity during the construction of the transcontinental railroad and was brought in by trainload.*

Right: *By April 1869, the Central Pacific construction crews had reached Utah and were drawing close to the meeting point at Promontory.*

Far right: *A plaque commemorates the day on which a record-breaking length of track was laid by Central Pacific construction crews. The rail layers seen in the foreground of the bottom photo were followed by gangs of Chinese laborers who spaced and spiked the rails to the ties.*
   Ties were spaced along the graded roadbed for some distance ahead and rails hauled to strategic spots. Work started at sunrise, and when darkness called a halt, the men discovered that the gang of eight Irish rail layers, backed by a small army of trackmen, had completed more than 10 miles of track.

Left: *Chinese workers near the entrance to Summit Tunnel, 105 miles from the Sacramento terminus, in 1866.*

These pages: *On 10 May 1869, the last rails of the Union Pacific and the Central Pacific (now the Southern Pacific) were joined at Promontory, Utah. A train from the East and one from the West halted within a few feet of each other. A memorable scene was then enacted—a spike of California gold was driven, marking the completion of the first chain of railroads to span the American continent. This historic moment was captured by Captain Andrew Joseph Russell.*

The photo at right shows the scene from the perspective of looking toward the Union Pacific train. Many of the photos documenting the construction of the Union Pacific were taken by Alexander Gardner, who followed the construction crews of the Union Pacific as they progressed west from the Missouri River.

Below: *These reproductions of the Union Pacific's No 119 and the Central Pacific's* Jupiter *reenact the historic meeting 10 May 1869 at Promontory, Utah.*

Right: *The Golden Spike that united East with West.*

Far right: *A poster proudly proclaims the grand opening of the nation's first transcontinental railroad.*

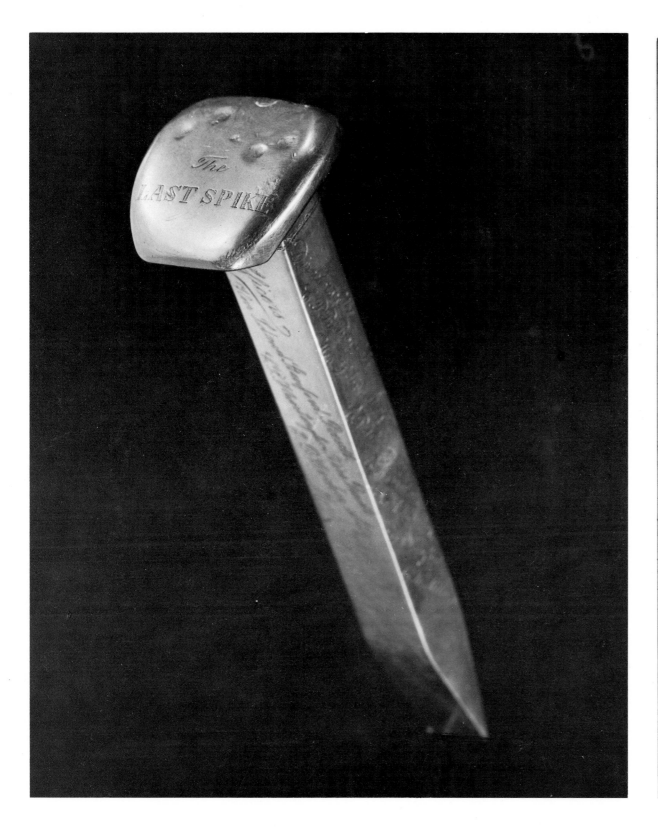

Below: Adorned with a set of antlers on its headlight, No 23 had been shined until every brass fitting gleamed to have its picture taken at the Wyoming Station, a small way stop on the Little Laramie River 15 miles west of Laramie. The engine was built by Schenectady Locomotive Works in 1868.

Left: *This steam shovel was needed to excavate the mountainous terrain at Hanging Rock in Echo Canyon, Utah during the building of the Union Pacific Railroad.*

Right: *A Union Pacific schedule from June 1868 and (far right) a poster urging farmers and mechanics to settle in the West.*

Below: *This exhibition train, which was assembled by the Union Pacific, closely resembles the first passenger train to run west from the Missouri River on the Union Pacific. The locomotive was built in 1870; car No 1, a combination mail, baggage and passenger car, in 1866; car No 9, a passenger coach; car No 97, one of the old emigrant sleepers, was purchased from the Pennsylvania Central Railroad in 1875; and car X01, an early business car, was built in 1883.*

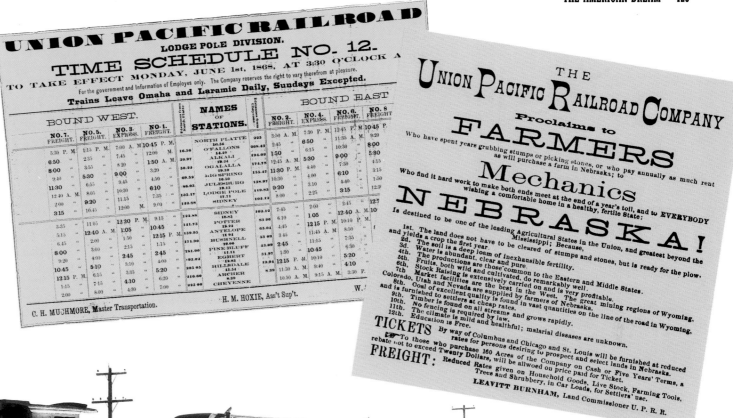

Above: *The first freight locomotive on the Denver & Rio Grande Western Railroad was the* Show-wa-no, *a 2-6-0 Mogul placed in service in 1871.*

Right: *The aftermath of a collision in Colorado, 1896. Despite appearances, the accident was not as serious as it seems, for it involved freight trains, not passenger trains.*

Left: *The first Union Pacific bridge across the Missouri River between Council Bluffs, Iowa and Omaha, Nebraska was a single track bridge with 11 spans measuring 250 feet each, for a total length of 2750 feet. It had a clearance of 60 feet above medium low water so that boats could pass under, and the roadway was not floored in order to accommodate wagon traffic. The bridge was opened for traffic on 14 March 1872. In 1882 it was removed to make way for a new double span track steel bridge.*

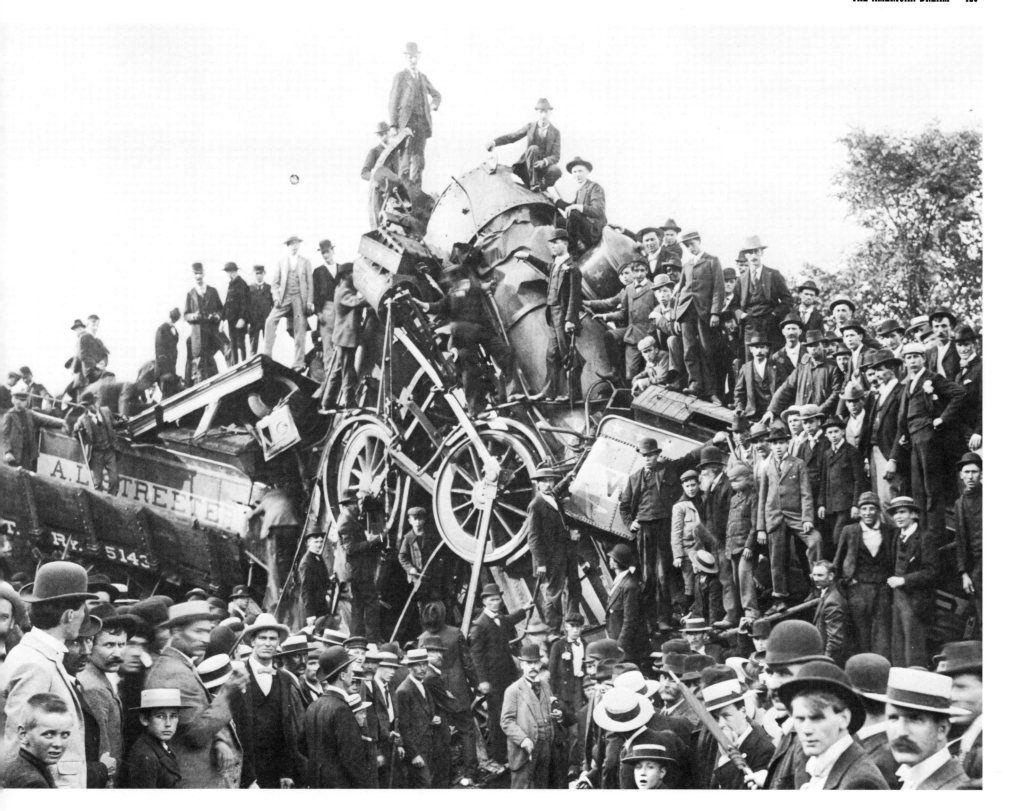

Previous pages: *This Currier & Ives engraving from 1872 portrays a locomotive and passsenger train crossing the plains, as a great fire rages in the distance.*

Below: *A Union Pacific camel locomotive built by Rogers of Paterson, New Jersey in 1887. The camel class of locomotives was designed by Ross Winans and first used on the Baltimore & Ohio in 1848. One of the most powerful locomotives of its time, it was also one of the most unusually designed locomotives ever built. The name 'camel' stemmed from the placement of the cab.*

Many of the small, local lines that once criss-crossed the western states were built in narrow gauge, usually three foot gauge, rather than standard gauge. Narrow gauge was cheaper to build particularly in the mountains, but the savings in construction were generally lost in the costs of off- and on-loading where the narrow gauge met the standard.

Although the locomotives used on these lines were smaller than those run on standard gauge, they were powerful enough to pull their loads up steep mountain grades. Steam locomotives used on the lines had a distinctive look. To improve stability, the frames were placed outside the wheels and the connecting rods drove on outside, separate cranks.

The Denver & Rio Grande Western was one of the largest narrow gauge lines and also one of the last to convert to standard gauge, continuing to operate narrow gauge on the commercial route from Alamosa to Farmington until 1967. Additionally, Denver & Rio Grande Western continued to operate the Durango-Silverton line (left) as a tourist attraction.

The photo at top shows a Denver & Rio Grande Western steam engine puffing across the stark, snow-covered flat land three miles west of Chama, New Mexico in 1968.

Today, a section of narrow gauge track that was once owned by the Denver & Rio Grande Western is now run by the State of Colorado. Called the Cumbres & Toltec Railroad (right), it operates as a tourist line.

Left: *Union Pacific No 4466 is now on display in Sacramento, a proud reminder of the days when steam ruled the rails.*

Below: *UP 2-8-2 No 1938 was used for local freight and switch work as well as for pusher service on the steep grade of the Missouri River Valley near Omaha.*

Above: *UP No 8444 was one of a proud group of 45 fast-stepping 4-8-4s passenger trains that flashed across the West. The last steam locomotive acquired by UP, No 8444—then known as 844—began operating in December 1944. During its distinguished career, No 8444 pulled the well-known* Overland Limited, Los Angeles Limited, Portland Rose *and* Challenger *trains on portions of their runs between Omaha and the West Coast and Pacific Northwest. Saved from the scrap pile in 1960, this locomotive has since been used for special service.*

Left: *Colorado & Southern 2-8-0 Consolidation No 634. The C&S was a Burlington Route subsidiary.*

Right: *During the 1870s, the CB&Q was essential to the farmers of the heartland, and in 1963 CB&Q No 5632 Northern was no less important to the people of Longmont County.*

Left: *This 0-6-0 switcher was an integral member of the Union Pacific stable—before the advent of the diesel engine.*

Left: *No 4019 is a* **Big Boy** *4-8-8-4 locomotive, the world's largest and most powerful steam locomotive. It was built for and used only on the Union Pacific. Tender and locomotive were 133 feet long and weighed 1,208,750 pounds. The 14-wheel tender had a capacity of 24,000 gallons of water and 22,000 pounds of coal per hour.*

Right: *The Challenger 4-6-6-4 type locomotive was second in size only to the* **Big Boy.** *Designed by Union Pacific and built by American Locomotive Company, the Challenger was the fastest and most versatile freight locomotive owned by the railroad. No 3985 is still used for special events.*

Left: *Leaving a trail of smoke behind it, UP No 8444 makes its way through the rugged terrain of the western United States.*

Left: *On a clear, brisk autumn afternoon, No 3985 races across the Great Plains.*

Right: *No 4003, one of UP's* **Big Boys,** *leaves Emkay, Wyoming in 2958. The* **Big Boys** *were capable of pulling a 3500-ton capacity load over the mountains. The locomotive's articulated construction allowed it to bend while rounding curves. This was a necessity because of the engine's extreme length.*

THE FAR WEST

Any discussion of great railroads of the Far West begins with mention of the four Sacramento, California shopkeepers who would be known as the 'Big Four.' These men—Charles Crocker, Collis Huntington, Mark Hopkins and Leland Stanford—chartered the Central Pacific Railroad in 1861 to build the western half of North America's first transcontinental railroad.

Before the Big Four, however, there was Theodore Dehone Judah, a civil engineer from Troy, New York who arrived in Sacramento in 1854 at the behest of the Sacramento Valley Rail Road Company (SVRR). With the Sacramento business community behind it, the SVRR had been incorporated in 1852 with plans for a railroad to connect that city with the gold fields of the Sierra, and Judah was the man picked to engineer the line. He was prepared to do the job, but his vision was fixed on a larger idea: a transcontinental line that would connect California to the rest of the nation.

His first western railroad complete, Judah became one of the leading exponents of a transcontinental, or 'Pacific,' railroad as it was known then. When Asa Whitney first suggested such a railroad in 1845, his was a decidedly minority voice. However, by the time Theodore Judah arrived in Washington, DC, in late 1856 to lobby Congress for funding, the idea had grown in popularity. Senator Thomas Hart Benton of Missouri had placed the idea before Congress in 1849, and Pacific railroad conventions had been held in Memphis, New Orleans and Boston that same year. It seemed as though the gold rush had won many converts to the dream of a railroad to the West.

In Sacramento, meanwhile, Theodore Judah had been introduced to the Big Four and on 28 June 1861 they formed the Central Pacific Railroad, forerunner of the empire that would be called the Southern Pacific. The Central Pacific was incorporated under the laws of California and dedicated to building a railroad across the Sierra via Dutch Flat. Leland Stanford became president of the new firm and Collis Huntington became its vice-president. The frugal Mark Hopkins was treasurer. Judah became chief engineer and Charles Crocker formed Charles Crocker and Company, a wholly owned subsidiary that would undertake construction of the Central Pacific.

On October 1861, having spent his summer in the Sierra, Theodore Judah reported to the directors of the Central Pacific that a practical route had been found. A year later, President Abraham Lincoln signed the Pacific Railroad Act that would call on the Central Pacific to build from the West and which created the Union Pacific to build the transcontinental from the East.

On 8 January 1863 Governor Leland Stanford, wielding a silver spade, broke ground at Front and K streets in Sacramento, and the dream was on its way to becoming a reality. After Theodore Judah completed his surveys and as the railroad was gradually built westward, Judah's role began to diminish. Though he still referred to it as 'my little road,' it clearly belonged to the four 'associates' who were financing and building it. Animosity developed between Judah and Huntington, so Judah decided to go east to seek the financing necessary to buy out his partners. He arranged a series of meetings in New York and left San Francisco by steamer in October 1863. When he crossed through the jungles of Panama, he contracted yellow fever, and on 2 November he died in New York at the age of 38.

On 7 October 1863 the Central Pacific's first locomotive arrived in Sacramento. On 9 November, having been dubbed *Governor Stanford*, it made its first run. On 25 April 1864 the first Central Pacific passenger service to Roseville began, and by 3 June the line had been extended to Newcastle. As the line reached into the mountains, the going became more difficult.

The Sierra Summit tunnels, begun even before the tracks reached Cisco, took two painful years to complete. These years, 1866 to 1868, included the two worst winters on record; men who weren't maimed in nitroglycerine mishaps ran the risk of freezing.

In July 1868 the Central Pacific had finally broken out of the mountains, and Charles Crocker stared in relief and anticipation at the relative flatness of Nevada.

The final mad dash was on. On 10 May 1869, the Central Pacific locomotive *Jupiter* moved toward Promontory, Utah, pulling the private car of Leland Stanford. On the track ahead was the Union Pacific's No 119 with UP vice president TC Durant. Stanford had actually arrived on 8 May and had waited in the rain for two days while Durant was delayed. (His train had been kidnapped by some unpaid contractors and was held until the account was settled.)

The rain stopped as the two locomotives paused within sight of one another, and the last rail was put into place. This was followed by speeches and the presentation of a golden spike and another speech. Stanford responded with a speech. In place of the silver spade he had taken up in Sacramento six years before, he brandished a silver hammer. Telegraph lines that had been strung

Facing page: *No 1065, an early Central Pacific train hauling ties across the trestle over the Little Truckee River near Boca.*

parallel to the two railroads were poised to carry the news east to Omaha and Chicago, and west to Sacramento and San Francisco. Both the spike and the hammer were wired into the telegraph so the moment of their contact could send a tiny spark of electricity exploding across the nation, poised breathless for this monumental occasion.

A hush fell over the assembled crowd as Leland Stanford swung the silver hammer at the first gold spike. The hammer plunged downward toward the final notch in the steel belt that would bind the nation...and missed. Stanford's second blow connected, but it was anticlimactic. Having seen the first blow fall short, a telegraphic technician had tapped his key and the celebrations in Chicago and San Francisco had already begun.

After they met the Union Pacific at Promontory, Utah, in 1869 to complete the historic link, the Big Four spread their empire throughout the literally golden state of California.

On 25 September 1869, the Big Four purchased the Southern Pacific, with its hub in San Francisco, and consolidated all of their spreading empire under its umbrella. The following year the Central and Southern Pacific operations were merged, although a full merger did not take place for another 15 years, at which time the operations for the entire network came under the Southern Pacific name.

In 1883 the Southern Pacific's Sunset Route, connecting New Orleans to California by way of Texas was completed. By 1884 Southern Pacific owned every mile of standard gauge railroad in the state of California, a 4711-mile system radiating from the bustling San Francisco yards to the far corners of the state and 800 miles beyond. When the line connecting Portland, Oregon to the California network was completed in 1887, Southern Pacific's route map covered a quarter of the United States, an empire unparalleled by any other American railroad.

Right: *The* CP Huntington, *Central Pacific's third locomotive, was later renumbered as Southern Pacific's No 1. The engine is now preserved at the California State Railroad Museum.*

Left: *Central Pacific Locomotive No 1, the* Governor Stanford, *in the railroad's Sacramento yard along Front Street during construction about 1864. The locomotive was too light for heavy operations on the steep grades of the Sierra Nevada as Central Pacific, now Southern Pacific, built into the mountain reaches, and No 1 was soon delegated to local work as a Sacramento switch engine.*

The locomotive is one of two existing engines from the first transcontinental railroad and still appears much as it did in this photo by Alfred A Hart, official Central Pacific photographer.

As always, Hart's photos tell a story. To the right of the engine are many lengths of the 56-pound iron rail awaiting shipment to railhead.

The fireman standing in the center with a mallet in his hand has just filled the engine with wood and is conferring with the engineer, who consults his watch.

Central Pacific's legendary Big Four were four merchants who had come west in the wake of the gold rush to set up shop in California's capital. The men joined forces to build the Central Pacific across the Sierra Nevada. Facing page, from left: *Collis P Huntington served as vice-president; Leland Stanford as president; Charles Crocker as president of Charles Crocker and Company and as construction supervisor; and Mark Hopkins as treasurer.*

Left: *Chinese workmen, using pick and shovel, one-horse dump carts and black powder, carve their way through and over the granite Sierra Nevada, preparing the way for the 690 miles of rails of the Central Pacific from Sacramento, California to Promontory, Utah.*

Left: *Central Pacific patrons view the progress of the trans-Sierra tracks from an excursion train in 1867. By this time, construction had reached 57 miles beyond Sacramento.*

Above: *Theodore Judah was the driving force behind the nation's first transcontinental railroad. He persuaded the famed Big Four of Sacramento to launch the Central Pacific Railroad as the western portion of the transcontinental railroad. He died on 2 November 1963, before any portion of the Central Pacific was placed in operation.*

Left: *CP construction crews in the Sierra Nevada, working to fulfill the dream of Theodore Judah.*

Right: *Crews at work on the 90-foot high Secrettown trestle in the Sierra Nevada. This 1867 photo shows the meager tools with which the builders had to work in blasting a trail over and through the rugged mountains for the rails of the Central Pacific.*

Left: *This 1875 photograph shows section men turning out for work on the building of the Southern Pacific line in the Tehachapi Mountains just north of Los Angeles.*

Right: *A few locals gather at the first railroad station in Los Angeles, circa 1869.*

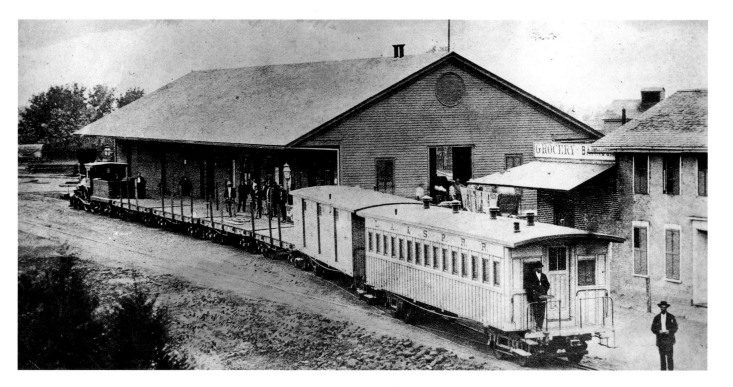

Right: *The San Gabriel was the first locomotive in Los Angeles County. This woodburner had a short life, beginning operations on 14 January 1869 on the Los Angeles & San Pedro Railroad, which was still under construction. The San Gabriel broke down before the railroad was completed and was scrapped in 1876.*

Above: *A way stop en route to Portland, Oregon. The first railroad in Oregon was established in 1865.*

Above, right: *An SP employee season ticket for 1888.*

Below: *A Southern Pacific passenger train pulls into the Monterey Station about 1882.*

Below: *In 1884, the CP shops at Sacramento built what was then the world's largest locomotive to haul loads over the Tehachapi Mountains in southern California. Built specifically at the request of Leland Stanford, El Gorbernador weighed 73 tons alone or 194.5 tons with a fully loaded tender. Its size was its undoing—the boiler was too small, and the engine was scrapped in 1894.*

Left: *Southern Pacific No 73, a 4-4-0 American-type locomotive, at the Monterey roundhouse in 1887.*

At first the Central Pacific purchased its engines and coaches from shops on the East Coast. The engines were disassembled, loaded onto sailing vessels, transported 15,000 miles around Cape Horn at the foot of South America to San Francisco, and then transferred to riverboats for the final leg up the delta to Sacramento. The time and expense involved in such a complicated process soon prompted the Big Four to set up a factory of their own in Sacramento.

In 1873, the first locomotive, No 173, rolled out of the shops. Until it closed in 1937, the Sacramento shops produced over 200 locomotives. The photo at right shows a group of workers from the Sacramento shops in 1889.

Below: *The roundhouse at the Sacramento shops in 1891.*

Right: *Life on a California logging railroad of the early 1900s. On board old No 3, engineer Mickey McCloud and fireman Tony Cooney haul a load of logs 12 miles to the mill on the Noyo River.*

Right: *Cars loaded down with giant redwood logs from California's northern coast head south to build the city of San Francisco.*

Facing page: *A work train hauls a contractor's flatcars on temporary tracks in Auburn, California, in the foothills of the Sierra Nevada.*

Above: *The Southern Pacific's* Overland Limited *approaches the 16th Street Station in Oakland. The photo was taken about 8 May 1908, when Admiral Bob Evans brought the American Battleship Fleet to San Francisco. The battleship* Iowa *can be seen in the bay.*

Left: *Southern Pacific 1320, a 4-4-0 built in 1882 by Schenectady, began life as Central Pacific No 104. It was renumbered No 1277 in 1891, before finally becoming No 1320 in 1901.*

Right: *Bedecked with flowers and flags, SP locomotive No 8 transported President William McKinley throughout the state during his visit to California in May 1901.*

Southern Pacific Company--Pacific System
COAST DIVISION

SPECIAL TIME TABLE

— FOR THE —

" PRESIDENT'S SPECIAL "

To take effect Friday, May 10, 1901, at 2 o'clock, P. M., and
void after 10 P. M., Tuesday, May 14, 1901

The " President's Special " will leave Santa Barbara May 10, 1901, and run
to San Francisco on the following time, and will have absolute right of track
over all trains, which must clear its time thirty minutes:

Friday, May 10

Leave Santa Barbara		Leave Hathaway Ave.	8.03 p. m.
" Irma	2.00 p. m.	" Goldtree	8.11 "
" Goleta	2.08 "	" Serrano	8.24 "
" La Patera	2.16 "	" Cuesta	8.36 "
" Coromar	2.19 "	" Santa Margarita	8.45 "
	2.23 "	" Havel	8.55 "
		" Atascadero	9.00 "
		" Asuncion	9.07 "
		" Templeton	9.14 "
		" Paso Robles	9.25 "
			9.36 "
			9.44

Left: *Even in the middle of the Mojave Desert, Santa Fe patrons could enjoy an excellent meal at Fred Harvey's Casa del Desierto in Barstow, California.*

Below: *The* Valley Flyer *builds up a head of steam for the next leg of its journey.*

Right: *The Sante Fe Depot in Los Angeles in the early twentieth century.*

Left: *The Southern Pacific locomotive erecting shops in Los Angeles. This 29 September 1924 photo shows a 200-ton crane lifting a 315,000-pound locomotive over other engines being repaired in the shops.*

Right: *The men perched on top of this engine reveal the true size of a powerful steam locomotive.*

Below: *A trainload of newly-built 2-10-2s leave the Baldwin Locomotive Works in Philadelphia in July 1922, heading west for duty with the Southern Pacific. Pictured beside the engine is Baldwin president Samuel Vauclain.*

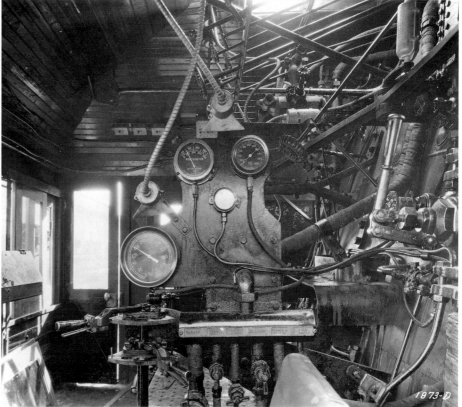

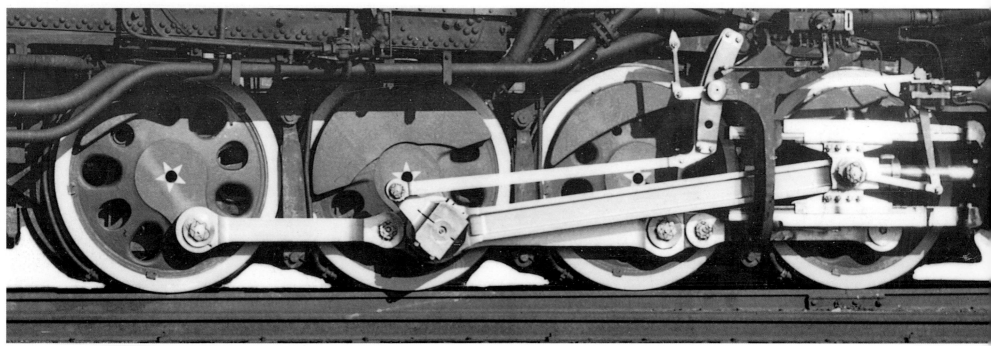

Far left: *A view of the engineer's side in a SP 4100 series locomotive. In the upper right hand is the throttle lever. The reverse lever and brake valves are to the right of the seat. The water glass and gauge cock are attached to the water column, seen in the upper left of the photo.*

Left: *The same cab as seen from outside the window on the fireman's side. In the lower left hand corner are the firing valve and damper regulator. Directly below is the steam gauge. The two other large gauges above are the feedwater heater and steam heat gauges.*

Right: *The 4100 series, of which No 4159 is an example, were known as cab forward (also cab-aheads or cab-in-front) locomotives. The cab, which was normally at the rear of the locomotive, was placed in front and the tender was moved to the rear. The cab forwards of the 1930s were the backbone of SP's mountain operations until they were replaced by diesels in the 1950s.*

Below: *The driving wheels of a typical Southern Pacific cab forward.*

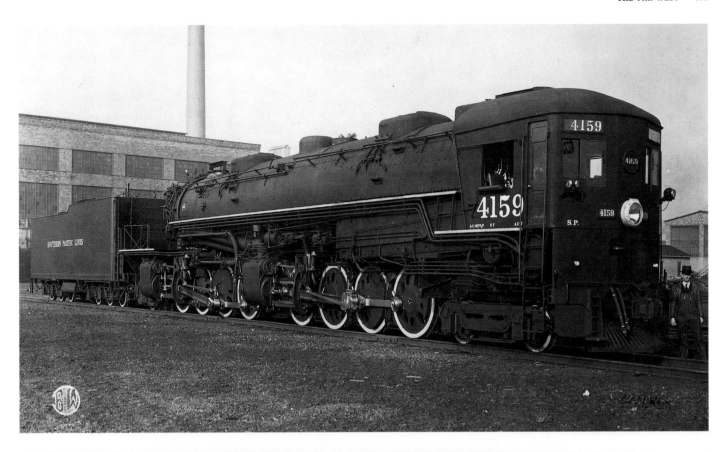

Below: *No 5000, an articulated locomotive with a 4-10-2 wheel configuration, was one of the many locomotives operating throughout Southern Pacific's vast network in the 1930s.*

These pages: *Southern Pacific No 4449 was one of the general service locomotives (class GS-2 through GS-4) placed in service in the late 1930s. After a decade of service on such streamline routes as the fabled* Coast Daylight, *these locomotives were retired.*

No 4449 was preserved, and in 1976 it was used to pull the Bicentennial Freedom Train. In 1984, repainted in original Daylight colors, No 4449 made a run from Portland to the New Orleans's World Fair. The photo at right by Vic Reyna captures No 4449 on that historic run.

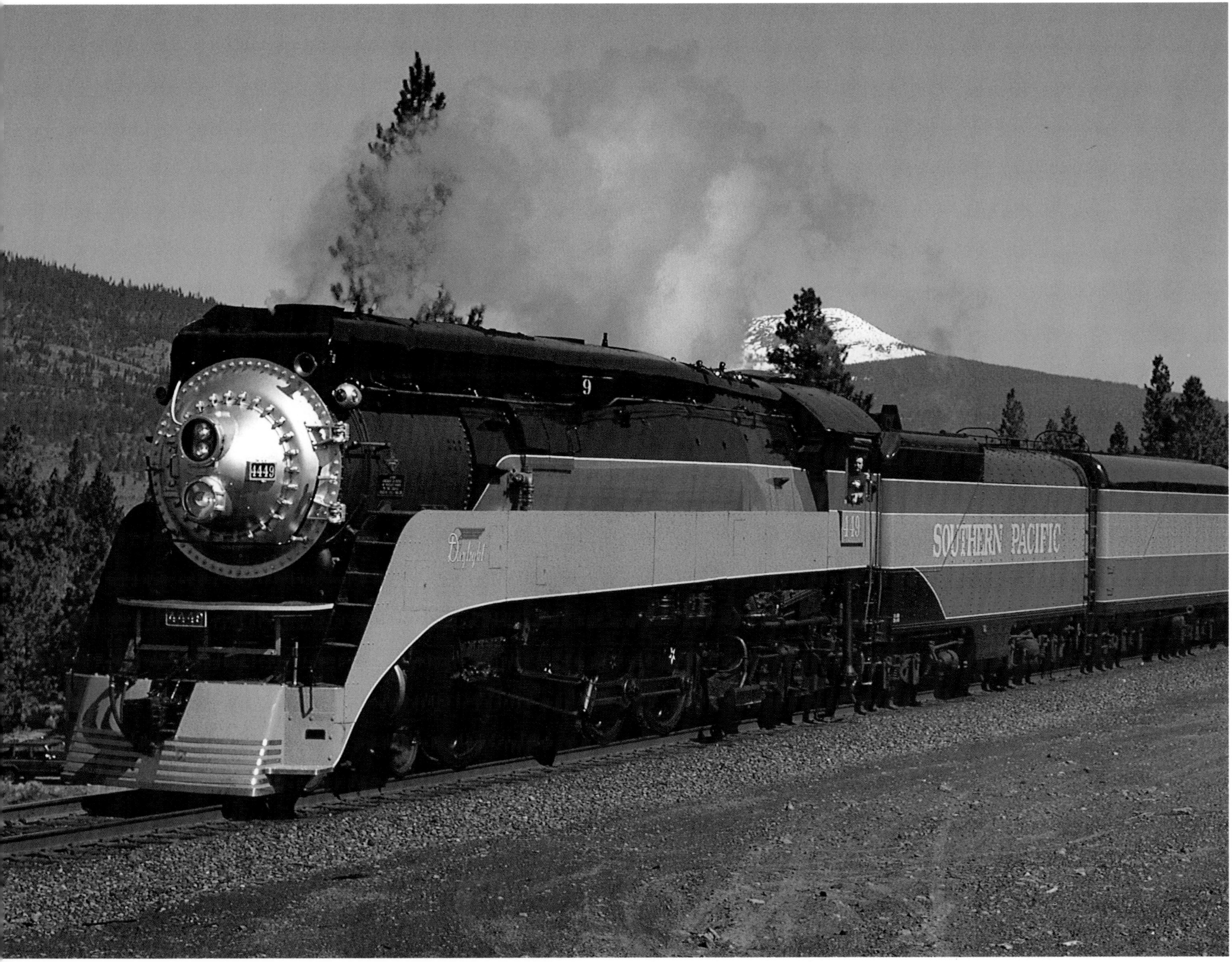
4449
SOUTHERN PACIFIC
Daylight
4449

During World War II, Southern Pacific, with routes extending from Portland to New Orleans, found itself with more military installations and embarkation points on its lines than any other railroad in the country.
Left: *Soldiers and the* Daylight's *engineer exchange greetings.*

Right: *Southern Pacific flat cars loaded with M-4 Sherman tanks in 1943.*

Below: *The SP transports a carload of soldiers.*

Below, right: *The San Luis Army Ordnance Depot.*

Left: *This California & Western 'Skunk' locomotive takes passengers on excursions through the redwoods of northern California. The C&W, which originated in the 1880s, operates between Fort Bragg and Willits, California.*

Right: *Southern Pacific No 1717 is now on display at Dunsmuir, California.*
Bottom caption

Right and above right: *Today a tourist train, the Felton, Big Tree & Pacific is the legacy of a Santa Cruz narrow gauge logging route.*

Right: *In recent years, small steam railroads, such as the Sierra Railroad, have flourished as tourist attractions. The Sierra Railroad dates back to 1897, when it connected the mines and lumber mills of Tuolumne County, California with the rest of the state. The old roundhouse (below right) at Jamestown continues to house steam locomotives and rolling stock that served the railway in its early days.*

Left: *No 483 of the Virginia & Truckee Railroad pulls a freight across a trestle.*

Below: *With awe written across their young faces, two boys enjoy the opportunity to inspect a locomotive.*

These pages: *Their days of glory long past, these old, abandoned steam locomotives serve as reminders of the golden age of railroading.*

THE NORTHWEST PASSAGE

In the sixteenth century, soon after it was learned that Christopher Columbus had *not* reached the East Indies, European explorers began searching for a way around the land mass of North America, a 'Northwest Passage' from the Atlantic to the Pacific. By the time of the American Revolution in 1776, the existence of a Northwest Passage was generally regarded as improbable—yet the dream lived on.

The idea of building a transcontinental, or 'Pacific' railroad was first seriously promoted by Dr Samuel Bancroft Barlow in 1834 and by John Plumb in 1836. A possible rail route following the path followed by Merriweather Lewis and William Clark's 1804-1806 expedition was surveyed by Asa Whitney in 1845. Senator Thomas Hart Benton of Missouri introduced the idea to Congress in 1849, and Pacific Railroad conventions were held in Memphis, New Orleans and Boston that same year. It seemed as though the 1849 California Gold Rush had won many converts to the dream of a railroad link to the West.

The only question, apparently, was that of what route the new road would take. The central route to the Pacific followed the major overland routes of the day and was the shortest, straight-line distance between San Francisco and chief western embarkation points like St Louis and Kansas City. Advocates of a northern route—the Lewis and Clark route—pointed out that the nature of the navigable Mississippi/Missouri River network made the Puget Sound 700 miles closer than San Francisco in terms of track that would have to be laid.

Signed into law in 1862 by President Abraham Lincoln, the Pacific Railroad Act called for *two* companies to undertake the task of constructing the new line. In the West was the Central Pacific Railroad, founded independently in 1861 by Leland Stanford, Collis Huntington, Charles Crocker and Mark Hopkins—the Big Four—to build a rail line across the Sierra Nevada to connect with the rails from the East, that they correctly assumed would soon be completed. From the East these tracks would be built by the federally chartered Union Pacific.

Since no site for a meeting point had been specified, a competition between the two began, which culminated with their meeting at Promontory, Utah, north of the Great Salt Lake, on 10 May 1869. The nation torn apart North and South by the Civil War was now bound together East and West by bands of steel.

A dream had been fulfilled, but the idea of the *northern* route—the true Northwest Passage—had not been abandoned. On 2 July 1864, just two years after he had signed the original Pacific Railroad Act and five years before the rails would link at Promontory, Utah, Abraham Lincoln signed an Act of Congress creating the Northern Pacific Railroad Company. Its eastern terminus was on Puget Sound and much of its route would follow the trail originally blazed by Lewis and Clark on their expedition.

The completion of the Northern Pacific came on 8 September 1883 at Gold Creek, Montana, before an audience that included distinguished guests from the United States, Germany, England and the Scandinavian countries. Witnessing the ceremony were cabinet officials, 10 United States senators and three former senators, 20 congressmen, four former congressmen, nine governors, four ex-governors and 25 of the nation's top railroad executives. The ceremonial 'last spike' was driven by former United States President Ulysses S Grant. It was not a gold spike, but rather the same steel spike used 13 years earlier to mark the beginning of construction near Carleton, Minnesota.

However, of all the railroads of the great northwest, one stands out, regal and aloof like the Rocky Mountain goat that it took as its emblem. The Great Northern was founded by James Jerome Hill, known and remembered as 'The Empire Builder.' In 1912, upon retiring, he said: 'Most men who have really lived have had, in some shape, their great adventure. This railway is mine.'

In 1881, Hill had acquired the Minneapolis & St Cloud Railway for $30,000. Chartered in 1856, the Minneapolis & St Cloud existed only on paper. In a quarter of a century it had built no track, yet it held very broad charter rights, an asset which James J Hill would bring into play eight years later. In 1886 the main line of the St Paul, Minneapolis & Manitoba was extended westward from Devil's Lake to Minot in Dakota Territory, to set the scene for one of the great epochs of railroad construction. Between April and mid-October 1887, 545 continuous miles of line, reaching across largely unsettled wilderness all the way from Minot to Great Falls in Montana Territory, was graded, bridged and laid with track.

On 18 September 1889 the name of the Minneapolis & St Cloud was changed to Great Northern Railway Company. On 1 February 1890 the new Great Northern

Facing page: This 1867 photo by CE Watkins shows the boat terminal and train on the portage railroad on the Washington side of the Columbia River. The block house where railroad workers sought safety from Indian attacks can be seen on the hill in the upper left of the photo.

took over the properties of the St Paul, Minneapolis & Manitoba, which actually had a smaller land grant than the anonymous Minneapolis & St Cloud.

The Rocky Mountains loomed ahead, and beyond, the Pacific. John F Stevens, a locating engineer later responsible for the Panama Canal, was hired to determine the easy, low-altitude route over the Rocky Mountains. He found Marias Pass, at the headwaters of the Marias River in Montana.

Construction of Great Northern's Pacific Coast extension began early in April 1890 at Pacific Junction, four miles west of Havre in what now was the fledgling state of Montana. Between here and Puget Sound lay 815 miles of mostly wild and rugged mountain land. Except for the town of Spokane, it was virtually uninhabited. For 430 miles, the route ran through heavy timber, and for more than 200 miles there was no sign of a trail. The heights of the Cascades had to be scaled by a switchback.

At the close of 1892, less than three years since Havre, only a seven-mile gap remained in what was once referred to as 'Hill's Folly.' On 6 January 1893, in the towering Cascades near Scenic, Washington, the final spike was driven by 'The Empire Builder.'

The Panic of 1893 swept a quarter of the nation's railroad mileage into receivership. Hill's first effort was to unify the operations of the Great Northern and the Northern Pacific. Although he was unable to merge the two roads, Hill did in fact take control of the Northern Pacific, and in 1901, he finally was able to arrange for the purchase by the Great Northern and the Northern Pacific of 97.2 percent of the outstanding stock of the Chicago, Burlington & Quincy Railroad, giving the parent lines access not only to Chicago but to the markets of the Midwest and South as well. Together again, the 'two' Northerns' created the Spokane, Portland & Seattle Railway—'The Northwest's Own'—in 1905. It was these four principle entities that came together to form Burlington Northern on 2 March 1970.

Right: On 28 June 1862, the William Crooks, *the first steam locomotive in the Northwest, chugged out of St Paul on its initial passenger run to the village of St Anthony (now Minneapolis).*

The Chicago, Burlington & Quincy, part of James J Hill's empire, would one day merge with the Northern Pacific and the Great Northern to form the Burlington Northern. No 27, Greyhound *(below), an American 4-4-0, was one of the CB&Q's earliest locomotives.*

Northern Pacific's first locomotive, the balloon-stacked Minnetonka *is still workin' on the railroad more than a century after it began service. Built in Pittsburgh by Smith and Porter at a cost of $6600, the 12-ton, 27.5-foot engine was delivered to the NP in 1870 and saw front-line duty with construction forces in both Minnesota and Washington. It was subsequently sold to a logging company on the Olympic Peninsula in western Washington.*

In 1932, Northern Pacific discovered the old wood-burner in retirement and brought it to St Paul, completely refurbishing it for the Chicago World's Fair in 1933-1934.

Today, the Minnetonka *continues to be exhibited on special occasions by Burlington Northern as a symbol of railroading's contribution to the development of the West.*

The photo at right *shows the* Minnetonka *on a bridge near Olympia, Washington in the early 1880s, while the photo on the* far right *shows the engine pulling two logging trucks.*

Right: *Chinese laborers at work on the Northern Pacific in the 1880s. Due to the scarcity of labor following the Civil War, Northern Pacific turned to Chinese workers for help building the first northern transcontinental line. These men, along with 10,000 white laborers, completed the railroad that spanned from the Pacific Coast to Minnesota.*

Right: *The first train crossed the Missouri River in March 1879 on tracks laid over the ice.*

Below: *The Minneapolis Terminal of the St Paul & Pacific RR in 1874.*

Left: *Henry Villard (seated with hat and cane) and a group of unidentified men. Villard became president of Northern Pacific in 1881 and during his tenure the NP line was completed.*

Below: *The Last Spike ceremony celebrating the completion of the Northern Pacific in September 1883 at Gold Creek, Montana. Henry Villard, president of NP, is seen standing on the locomotive.*

Above: *Northern Pacific No 225, a 4-4-0 was built in 1883.*

Left: *Baldwin Locomotive Works built this 2-8-0 for Northern Pacific in 1889.*

Right: *The William Crooks, a balloon-stack American built by Smith & Jackson at Paterson, New Jersey, arrived in St Paul in 1861 on a Mississippi riverboat. The No 1 locomotive for the St Paul & Pacific, Great Northern's original predecessor line, it was named for its chief engineer.*

Below: *The historic arrival of the first passenger train, NP No 41, at Minnewakon, North Dakota on 10 August 1885.*

Right: *A Great Northern locomotive crosses Two Medicine Bridge, near the boundary of present-day Glacier National Park, just east of the crossing of the Continental Divide at Marias Pass.*

During 1887 pioneer rail-laying gangs (left) *built 642 miles of track on the St Paul, Minneapolis & Manitoba Railway, beginning at Minot in Dakota Territory and concluding at Helena in Montana Territory. Along the way the men established four records for speed in construction.*

The photo on the left *shows the workers as they move up the railhead, accompanied by soldiers for protection from hostile Indians. The 'Skyscraper' dormitory cars had to be sawed down to tunnel size when the rails reached the mountains.*

Right: *Rogers Locomotive and Machine Works built this 2-6-0 for St Paul, Minneapolis & Manitoba Railway in 1887.*

Laying Steel into Whitefish.

Facing page: *Construction crews at White-fish, Montana lay steel for rails, circa 1903.*

Left: *Jim Hill drives the golden spike at Bend, Oregon on 5 October 1911, celebrating the completion of the Oregon Trunk Railway.*

Right: *James J Hill—the Empire Builder. Hill's purchase of the St Paul & Pacific in 1878 was the first step toward building his railroad empire.*

Below: *Baldwin Locomotive Works developed the N class Mallet-type (compound) 2-8-8-0 articulated locomotives in 1912. Between 1925 and 1927, the original N-1's, 25 in all, were made into simple articulated engines, modernized and reclassified as N-2's.*

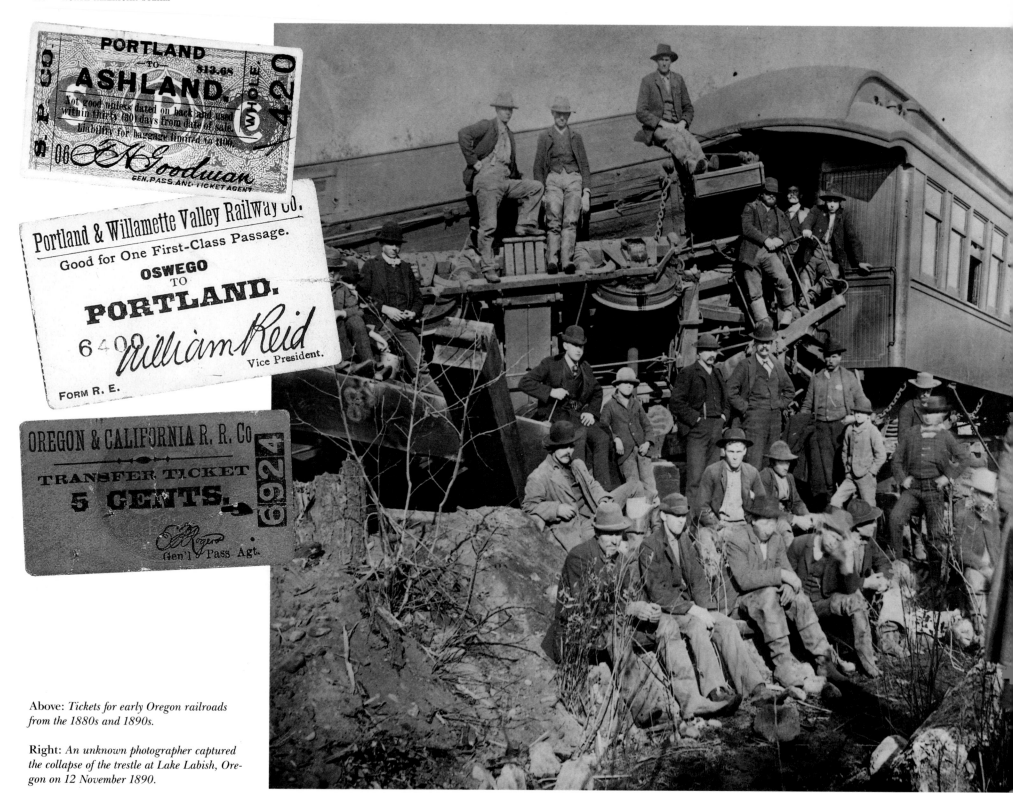

Above: *Tickets for early Oregon railroads from the 1880s and 1890s.*

Right: *An unknown photographer captured the collapse of the trestle at Lake Labish, Oregon on 12 November 1890.*

Below: *Main and Front streets in Medford, Oregon during the 1880s. To the left is the first Southern Pacific station. The railroad began serving Medford on 25 February 1884. On the right is the Riddle House, which was later remodeled and renamed the Nash Hotel.*

Right: *Three locomotives hauling a passenger train pull into Medford in 1910.*

Far left: *Southern Pacific 10-wheeler No 2193 at Canby, Oregon shortly after the turn of the century. No 2193 was one of AJ Stevens' famous 'monkey motion' engines equipped with his revolutionary valve gear. A pipe emerged from the steam dome, ducked behind the boiler and protruded from behind the smokebox to a position above the old 'hen-coop' pilot. The purpose of this design was to supply steam to the pile driver or steam shovel that was attached to the work train. Early work equipment had no boilers of their own and depended on the work train to supply them.*

Far left, below: *Northwestern Pacific No 112 was used well into the twentieth century.*

Below: **Big Jack**, *the locomotive for the Whitney Company, an Oregon logging company.*

Left: *Chicago, Burlington & Quincy 4-4-0 No 148 at the 12th Street Station in Chicago, circa 1893.*

Right: *Chicago, Burlington & Quincy No 35, a 4-4-0, was built in 1892. The locomotive was restored in Denver in 1932 for the Chicago World's Fair the following year.*

Below: *Chicago, Burlington & Quincy No 520, a Baldwin-built 0-6-0 in the yards with passenger cars, circa 1921.*

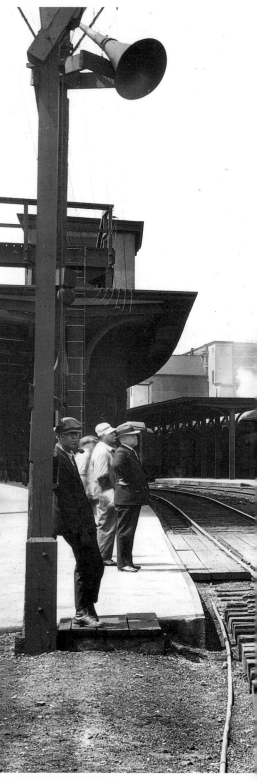

Great Northern's Empire Builder—*one of the great name trains of all time—is shown below at the St Paul Union Depot on the day of its inaugural run, 11 June 1929. The $5 million fleet of eight luxury trains cut five hours from previous schedules between Chicago and Seattle, making the run in 62 hours and 45 minutes.*

In 1947, Great Northern introduced the nation's first post-war fleet of streamliners, continuing the Empire Builder *tradition. A completely new fleet of streamlined* Empire Builders *went into service in 1951.*

Left: *The* Empire Builder *races through the Rockies.*

Below: *A carrier of iron ore from the mines of northeastern Minnesota to ports on Lake Superior, the Duluth, Missabe & Iron Range is descended from a number of smaller iron-carrying lines of the region. The railroad was purchased by US Steel in 1901 and to this day remains the nation's largest carrier of iron ore in the United States. In recent years, however, as the supply of high-grade ore has diminished, the line has carried more taconite, a low-grade ore that is processed into pellets.*

Left: *In 1910, Baldwin built a series of 2-6-8-0 Mallet Articulateds, such as No 1959, for Great Northern.*

Below: *Northern Pacific No 1836, a 2-8-2. Baldwin referred to 2-8-2s as Mikados because the first ones were built for export to Japan.*

Right: *A trio of Great Northern giants at Appleyard, near Wenatchee, Washington in 1958 —(from left to right) a 5000- horse-power single-cab electric, a 5400-horsepower four-unit diesel-electric and a 2-8-8-2 oil-burning steam locomotive.*

Below right: *The driving wheels on a 2-10-2 Santa Fe-type locomotive. Great Northern used the 2-10-2 for heavy freight service.*

ACROSS CANADA

With the second largest land area of any nation on earth, Canada possesses a vastness which could, in the nineteenth century, be brought into human scale only by rail transport. Indeed, this huge and rugged country was first defined as a nation by its railways.

Canada is today home to only two railways—Canadian National and Canadian Pacific—that truly span the entire North American continent. They each cover roughly 75 degrees of the earth's circumference, while Australia's continent-spanning India Pacific and America's great Southern Pacific span barely 35 degrees. Even the great Trans Siberian Railway in the Soviet Union—the longest railway in the world—spans only 85 degrees. As in the Russian Empire of the nineteenth century, Canada's vast horizons cried out for the power of steel rails to bind its cities, outposts and wilderness into a single great civilization. The tiny Champlain & St Lawrence Railroad Company, the first of the building blocks that would become CN, was the first-ever steam railway in the country, making its maiden run in 1836.

Still, however, the dream of spanning the great land remained. In 1851 Allan MacDonnell of Toronto sought a charter and a subsidy for a railroad to the Pacific, and the Canadian authorities, in declining, expressed their opinion that the scheme was not visionary and their hope that some day Great Britain and the United States might undertake it jointly.

Two things were needed before dreams on paper could become facts in steel—national unity and international rivalry. After Confederation in 1867, all speed was made to buy out the sovereign rights of the Hudson's Bay Company. Then came the first Riel Rebellion to bring home the need of a western road, as the *Trent* affair had brought home the need of the *Intercolonial*. The decisive political factor came into play in 1870, when British Columbia entered the federation.

If Canada was to become a strong, progressive and united country, a network of railways to bind it together—from the eastern provinces to the Pacific Ocean, from the arctic wastelands to the fertile prairies—was necessary. When the last spike of the Canadian Pacific Railway was driven at Craigellachie, British Columbia, on 7 November 1885, Canada gained a new world image and a new sense of identity. This new railway was more than just two ribbons of steel—it was an instrument of national unity, and later a source of friction.

Canadian National is just as much a part of Canadian history. While there were nearly 90 railway companies in Canada at the turn of the century, the three transcontinental systems—the Canadian Northern, the Canadian Pacific and the Grand Trunk—controlled more than 80 percent of the total mileage and also owned a variety of subsidiary undertakings such as steamships, hotels, express service, irrigation and land development and grain elevators. The control by Canadian railways of seven or eight thousand miles of lines in the United States, with corresponding extensions into Canada by American lines, was an outcome of geographic conditions, intimate social and trade connections, and a civilized view of international relations which no other countries could match.

Sir Robert Borden, who had become prime minister in 1911 argued for public ownership of a nationwide railway system. He pointed out that 90 percent of the Grand Trunk's transcontinental ambitions were already publicly funded by government loans, and for only 10 percent more the country could own and control the system. Faced by the urgent demands of World War I, Parliament decided to act on his suggestion.

It began in 1917 by obtaining the Canadian Northern and appointing a board of directors chaired by DB Hanna. The following year, the board's jurisdiction was extended over the Canadian Government Railways, 15 lines in all, the main ones being the Intercolonial, the National Transcontinental, the Hudson Bay Railway and the Prince Edward Island Railway.

Then on 6 June 1919, Parliament passed an Act incorporating the Canadian National Railway Company and appointed Hanna as president. The first major acquisition made by the new corporation was of the Grand Trunk Pacific the following year.

When the Government of Canada incorporated Canadian National, it created one of the largest railways in the world with various railway-related services operated for the benefit of its sole shareholder—the people of Canada. It had 105,905 employees and 2078 pensioners. From the many companies assembled in it came 3268 locomotives pulling 138,925 cars of various types along more than 21,700 miles of track, and also telegraph lines, hotels, steamships, car ferries, barges and tugs. The Canadian National was now and forever Canada's largest railway.

Facing page: *Canadian Pacific crews at work in the lower Fraser Valley in 1883. The railroad ties, piled on flatcars, are being unloaded and carried forward on the shoulders of the tracklayers.*

The Great Western was one of Canada's earliest and most successful railroads. In 1855, GW built the first railway suspension bridge (left) connecting Canada with the United States. An engineering marvel, it spanned the Niagara River just below the Falls and was 820 feet long.

Right: *Great Western officials pose with the* William Weir, *an early wood-burning locomotive.*

Below: *Built for Canada's Intercolonial Railway, this locomotive was the first one to come out of the shops at Moncton, New Brunswick.*

Above: *The first locomotive in the Canadian west arrived in Winnipeg, Manitoba on 9 October 1877. The stern-wheeler* Selkirk *pushed a barge laden with the locomotive, conductor's van and six flatcars.*

Flags waved in the breeze as the stern-wheeler's crew and deckhands posed for their picture on the third flatcar, to the left of the tender.

The locomotive's owner, Joseph Whitehead, named it the Countess of Dufferin, *in honor of the wife of the Governor-General. The proud designation CPR No 1 appeared on the engine and the tender and rolling stock bore the words Canadian Pacific, even though the CPR company was still over three years in the future. Today, the* Countess of Dufferin *is on display in Winnipeg (left).*

In 1883, William Cornelius Van Horne, the general manager of the Canadian Pacific, assembled 12,000 men, 5000 horse and 300 dog teams to build the railroad along Lake Superior. This land, untraveled by whites, offered little to sustain life. Twisted rocks, numerous lakes, fast-running streams and thick forests made passage on foot difficult. Bitterly cold in winter, the region turned into a swamp in summer when the heat and mosquitoes tormented man and beast alike.

Left: *A group of workers, known as navvies, pose in front of their tents at their construction camp, north of Lake Superior.*

Right: *A newly excavated rock cut along the north shore of Lake Superior.*

Left: *Workmen survey their handiwork at Morrison's Cut during the construction of the Canadian Pacific in 1884.*

Above: *A government-built timber trestle near the Lake of the Woods. This structure is typical of the flimsy, non-standard construction which was tolerated on government contracts. When the Canadian Pacific took over the Lakehead-Winnipeg section between 1881 and 1883, such structures were replaced with earth fills.*

Right: *A primitive piledriver at work in the Nicola River trestle in 1884. The barren hills of the upper Thompson Valley can be seen in the background.*

Right: *The famed tracklaying machine in operation. In reality, it was not a machine but a delivery gantry that carried rails forward in troughs along one side of the lead car and its support cars, while ties were moved forward in the same manner on the opposite side. The troughs were attached to the stake pockets on the sides of the flatcars. As the supply of rails was depleted, the troughs could be readily transferred to loaded cars.*

Right: *This photo sums up many of the frustrations encountered by the CP in the muskeg area, or bogs, northwest of Port Arthur. The track was built under government contract before the Canadian Pacific arrived in the area. Because the rails were laid on an embankment across a body of water, the tracks were unsafe for passenger and freight trains, and the CP was required to redo much of the previous work.*

Above: *This photograph shows one of six tunnels constructed in the Cherry Creek bluffs. The south shore of Kamloops Lake was a region of deep coves marked by these rocky buttresses.*

Left and right: *No structure on Canada's first transcontinental railroad equalled the Mountain Creek Bridge in size, location or symmetry. Located on the eastern slope of the Selkirks, the bridge was 164 feet in height, 1086 feet long and contained over two million board feet of timber.*

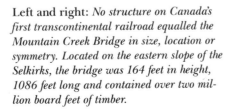

Above: *Canadian Pacific workers extend a timber retaining wall near Eleven Shed in Rogers Pass.*

Right: *Probably Canada's most famous photograph, this picture was taken on 7 November 1885 at 9:22 AM, Pacific time at Eagle Pass, British Columbia. The Honorable*

Donald Smith of the CPR is driving the last spike to complete the Canadian Pacific Railway transcontinental mail line between the Atlantic and Pacific oceans.

Far right: *William C Van Horne, the general manager of the CPR. His drive and vision took the CPR across the continent.*

Right: *The CPR station at Lethbridge, Alberta, as it appeared in 1899. Many of the lonely stations on the prairies would become the nuclei of new communities, dependent on the railway for their livelihood.*

Left: *In a recreation of the past, a vintage locomotive chugs across the Canadian prairie in the documentary 'National Dream.'*

Right: *The Canadian Pacific water tower at Fife, British Columbia.*

The way of life of the Plains Indians was for-ever altered by the building of the transconti-nental. Soon the buffaloes —-once the lifeblood of the Indian—would vanish from the plains. This photograph (left) from the late 1880s shows the bones of buffaloes loaded into a CP boxcar near Moose Jaw, Sas-katchewan to be used as fertilizer.

Below: Bedecked with flags and evergreens, the first transcontinental train arrives at Port Arthur, Ontario on 30 June 1886. Its arrival was greeted with much fanfare, as residents turned out in full force to inspect the luxu-rious sleepers and diners.

Below: *On a summer afternoon in 1900, a girl and her young charge await the arrival of the Canadian Pacific at the station in Vermillion Bay, Ontario. This vintage photograph was taken by Joseph W Heckman.*

Above: *CPR No 2524 prepares to pull out of Winnipeg, Manitoba, late in the afternoon on an August day in 1940.*

Right: *A CPR engineer and locomotive pause briefly at Abbotsford, British Columbia in March 1943.*

Facing page, top: *One of CPR's big 4-6-0s that were used until diesel locomotives reigned supreme. The photo on the* facing *page,* bottom *provides a close-up of the driving wheels on this type of locomotive.*

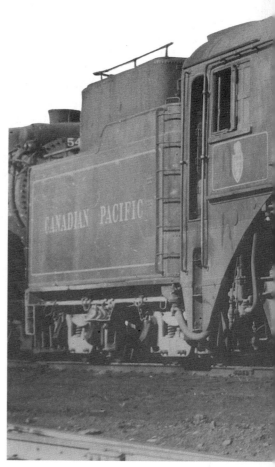

Left: *CPR No 2203 in Ontario in June 1942.*

Below left: *Row after row of boxcars line the freight yards at Saskatoon, Saskatchewan sometime in the 1930s.*

Below: *Locomotive 2716, a 4-6-2 G-5, was photographed in Vancouver, British Columbia in 1951.*

Left: *A group of Hungarian immigrants arrive at their new home, via the Canadian National. They were part of a huge influx of Europeans who immigrated to Canada in the 1920s.*

Left: *Passengers mill about the CPR station at Revelstoke, British Columbia on a hazy day in the 1920s.*

Right: *The Continental Ltd races through the Canadian Rockies as snow-capped Mt Robson rises majestically in the background.*

Left: Passengers on the Canadian Pacific Railway are treated to spectacular vistas, such as this one of Mt Cathedral. During its early years, the railroad counted on the awe-inspiring scenery of the Canadian West to encourage people to travel by rail.

Below: *Locomotives like this powerful steam engine were the backbone for the CPR passenger and freight service throughout a good part of the twentieth century.*

Right: *The sun sets on a CPR caboose at the yards at Midway, British Columbia.*

Below: *No 6218 of the Canadian National, now officially known as CN Rail. Canadian National Railways was established in 1922 to assume control of several financially distressed railways, including the Canadian Northern, Grand Trunk Railway and Grand Trunk Pacific.*

Left: *The sleek-lined CN No 6400, a 4-8-4 streamliner of the early 1940s. Though innovative, these steam locomotives would eventually be deposed by diesel engines.*

Right: *An early twentieth century CN 4-6-4 Hudson passenger locomotive.*

Below: *CN No 3430, a coal burning 2-8-2 Mikado-type locomotive. Mikados were used for heavy freight service.*

The last Canadian National steam locomotive
in regular service was CN No 6218, a 4-8-4
Northern class oil burner. No 6281 is seen
above crossing a trestle near Shawinigan,
Quebec on an exhibition run.

CN No 6157 (right) is also a 4-8-4 Northern. In its day, No 6157 was used for freight
service.

Today, CN Rails has replaced all its steam
locomotives with diesels and handles only
freight service. In 1978, passenger service
was taken over by Via Rail.

Left: *Canadian Pacific No 5924 pulls into the station at Banff, Alberta in 1948. Since the railroad was completed, vacationers have been drawn to Banff by its beautiful mountain scenery.*

Canadian Pacific No 5927, a Selkirk-type steam locomotive is seen at right hauling the trans-Canada passenger train, the Dominion, *along the Bow River in Alberta. The Selkirks were the largest and heaviest steam locomotives in the Commonwealth, boasting 10 63-inch (160 cm) drivers. No 5927 was built by the Montreal Locomotive Works in 1938 and was scrapped in December 1957.*

Left: *CPR 4-6-4 Royal Hudson No 2860 marches through Shannon, British Columbia on an exhibition run in June 1985. The engine was restored in 1974. The locomotives in this series were named Royal Hudson after the Royal Family toured Canada on No 2850 in 1939. Afterwards, these partially streamlined 4-6-4s were fitted with embossed crowns.*

Above: *In a vivid illustration of its history, six Canadian National engines line up at Belleville, Ontario for Railway Week.*

INDEX

Above: *Grand Trunk No 1084 and its crew pose for this photograph taken sometime around the turn of the century. Built by the Hinkley locomotive works in 1883, this 4-4-0 saw service until 1920, when it was scrapped.*

PICTURE CREDITS

All photos are from the AGS Picture Archives, with the following exceptions:

Albany Institute of History and Art, McKinney Library 15 (right, top and bottom)

Alco Historic Photos 20-21 (left), 24-25 (left), 29, 128-129

University of Arizona, Special Collections 89 (bottom), 94, 158 (top)

Association of American Railroads (AAR) 1, 14-15 (left), 22 (both), 32, 35, (both), 38 (top right and bottom), 45 (inset), 64-65, 68, 69 (bottom), 76, 178-179 (right), 180 (both), 186 (bottom)

Atchison, Topeka & Santa Fe Railway via AAR 85

Baltimore & Ohio Railroad Company via AAR 31, 33 (top), 36 (top left), 38 (top left)

Baltimore & Ohio Railroad Museum Archives 34, 36-37 (right), 60 (bottom)

BBC Hulton/Bettman Archive 125

Bison Picture Library 111 (bottom right), 183 (bottom), 190-191 (center)

HL Broadbelt Collection 26-27, 28 (bottom left), 33 (bottom), 39, 42 (top), 43 (both), 44 (top), 45, 52 (top), 52-53 (bottom), 55 (top), 56, 58 (bottom), 72-73, 162-163 (bottom), 163 (top), 198-199

California State Railroad Museum 9, 41, 44 (bottom), 48 (both), 49, 54, 55 (all)

University of California, Bancroft Library 145 (top, second and fourth), 154 (both), 155

Canadian Broadcasting Company 216

Canadian National Railway 204 (both), 205, 222 (bottom left), 224, 225, 228-229, 230, 231 (both), 232, 233, 237

Canadian Pacific Corporate Archives 203, 206-207 (both), 208 (both) 209, 210 (both), 211, 212-213 (all), 214-215 (all), 217 (top), 218 (both), 219, 224 (bottom), 234, 235

Chesapeake & Ohio Railway Historical Society 58 (top), 60 (top), 61

©Al Chione 131 (top), 139

Currier and Ives 11, 63, 126-127

Denver & Rio Grande Western Railroad via AAR 124 (top)

Golden Spike Productions 59m 118, 133 (bottom), 134, 135

Grand Trunk Western Railroad 40 (top), 46, 47 (top), 239

Great Northern Railway via AAR 186 (top)

©Nils Huxtable's Steamscenes 7, 50-51 (both), 74-75, 130, 132 (left), 134 (bottom), 137, 138 (bottom), 236

Kalmbach Publishing Company Photo Collection 12-13, 23

©V Lefter/FPG 131 (bottom)

Library of Congress 69 (top), 114-115 (center)

Michigan Department of State Archives 47 (bottom)

National Railway Historical Society 115 (top right), 177

New York Central System Historical Society, Purinton Collection 16-17 (both), 28 (top left)

New York Historical Society, New York City 18, 19, 23 (bottom), 25 (right)

Norfolk Southern Corporation 78, 79

Northern Pacific Railraod via AAR 181

Pullman Company via AAR 36 (bottom left)

©Vic F Reyna 166 (bottom), 167

©Ron Ruhoff's Photomusical Adventures 133 (top), 138 (top)

Santa Fe Southern Pacific Corporation 2-3, 4-5, 81, 82-83, 84 (both), 86, 87, 88, 90 (both), 91, 92-93, 95 (both), 96 (both), 97, 98-99 (both), 91, 92-93, 95 (both), 104 (both), 105, 106- 107 (all), 114 (left, top and bottom), 119 (left), 141, 142-143 (both), 144, 145 (top first and third, bottom), 146 (right), 148, 149 (both), 150 (top, left and right), 151, 152, 153 (both), 156 (both), 157 (both), 158 (bottom), 160, 161 (both), 162 (top left and right), 164-165, 166 (top right), 168, 169 (all), 173 (bottom left)

Seaver Center for Western History Research, Natural History Museum of Los Angeles County 89 (top), 100, 101 (both) 159

Smithsonian Institution 42 (bottom), 52 (bottom), 57 (bottom), 70 (both), 71 (both), 178 (left), 182 (both), 183 (top), 184 (both) 185 (top), 187 (bottom), 194, 195 (both)

Southern Methodist University, DeGolyer Library 40 (bottom)

Southern Pacific Company via AAR 115 (bottom right), 146 (left), 147, 150 (bottom)

Stan F Styles 217 (bottom), 220 (both), 221 (both), 222 (top left), 222-223 (right) 226-227 (all)

Union Pacific Corporation 136

Union Pacific Historical Collection 109

Union Pacifc Railroad via AAR 111 (top right), 113 (top), 116, 123 (bottom), 124 (bottom)

Union Pacifc Railroad Museum Collection 110-111 (left), 112, 113 (bottom), 117 (both), 120-121, 122, 123 (top left and right)

©Bill Yenne 166 (top left), 170, 171 (all), 174, 175 (all)

Below: *The* John Bull *of the Camden & Amboy Railroad. Built in England at the request of the American railroad pioneer Robert Stevens, the* John Bull *hauled its first passengers on 12 November 1831. Today, the* John Bull *can be seen at the Smithsonian Institution in Washington, D.C.*